Dr. Ava Cadell's
12 Steps To Everlasting Love

MW01141121

For information, contact:
Peters Publishing, PMB #161, 8033 Sunset Blvd., Los Angeles, CA 90046 • 310.276.8623

Library of Congress Catalog Card Number: 99-094511

ISBN 0-9662623-3-6

Cadell, Ava.
12 Steps To Everlasting Love: A Guide to Self-Improvement and Positive Relationships / Ava Cadell

Disclaimer

The author of this book does not provide medical advice nor prescribe the application of any of the activities and/or tasks recommended in the program as a substitute for or as a form of treatment for mental, emotional, physical or medical problems, without the advice of a trained therapist or physician.

The intent of the author is to offer guidance and information to help you in your quest for an everlasting love relationship. The purpose of the 30-Day Plan of Action workbook is to educate, motivate and document your own personal experiences.

The author and publisher shall have neither liability nor responsibility to any person or entity with respect to any loss or damage caused, or alleged to be caused, directly or indirectly, by the information contained in this book. Results as to the success of the program outlined herein are not guaranteed and are subject to individual application and effort.

Table of Contents

30 Day Plan of Action

Dr. Ava's 12 Steps To Everlasting Love

Preface

We've all been raised on fairy tales. Once upon a time, a young woman met her handsome Prince Charming, they fell madly in love, got married, had gorgeous children, and lived happily ever after.

But it doesn't happen quite like that, does it? The true story sounds something like, "Once upon a time, a woman fell in love with her Prince Charming, but it didn't quite work out; then she met another Prince Charming, and that didn't quite work out either, and again she met another Prince Charming, and guess what? It still didn't quite work out. Finally, she stopped and examined what she was doing, reevaluated what she wanted, and what was causing these heartbreaks. She wanted everlasting love, but something was stopping her from getting it. She wanted to find out what was missing.

Maybe she or he is reading these words right now!

Dr. Ava Cadell

"I would rather live and love where death is king than have eternal life where love is not."

Robert G. Ingersoll

Remember, it is always futile to try to control another person. You wind up either chasing rainbows or chewing up your fingernails in chronic anxiety. The only thing you can ever control for certain is your reaction to any situation. For instance, If a lover dumps you for someone else, don't dwell on it. Let someone else put up with your erstwhile lover, and think of how lucky you are to be free to find someone better.

Successful thought patterns, like everything in life that endures, are built up slowly, one by one. Take control over your "failure" thoughts. Visualize what you want until you believe in it, and go for it! After all, it is successful thoughts that motivate us; depressing thoughts stop us in our tracks. Each moment is precious to you in your search for everlasting love. You can't afford the luxury of a depressed mind if you want a fulfilling partnership. Say to yourself each evening: "What did I do with my beautiful day today that will guide me closer to the love I want?" You'll be surprised how creative your mind can become in searching out that right partner.

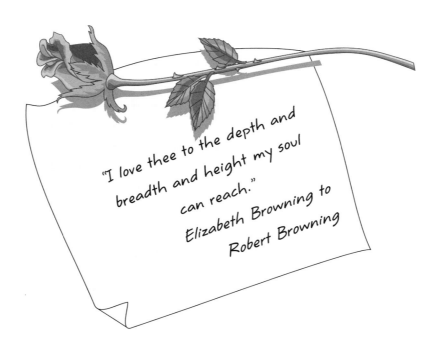

"I love thee to the depth and breadth and height my soul can reach."

Elizabeth Browning to Robert Browning

HOW TO USE THIS BOOK

Dr. Ava's 30-Day Plan of Action for Everlasting Love

I encourage each of you to go through the book step-by-step. As you read about each step, you can begin thinking of your goal and how far you have to go to reach it. The exercises listed with each chapter are designed for you to take at your own pace. The fastest you should be able to accomplish them is within 30 days; the slowest recommended pace is 12 months. If you take more than one year, you may be procrastinating about finding your everlasting love!

Please remember that each day is a new day for both opportunity and reflection. The steps you follow must become part of your daily routine. Only through continued reinforcement of your positive energy and thoughts can the goal become reality. You alone must make the effort; no one else can do it for you! If you have positive thoughts about the future, then positive things will happen for you.

You do not, however, have to go through the 12-step process by yourself. You can do it in small gatherings of friends or support groups. It is good to share these experiences with others who are also looking for their everlasting love. And don't become despondent if you can't accomplish everything by-the-book. These 12 steps are guidelines that can help you achieve your goal, but they are not rigidly etched in stone.

However, it is important to take one step at a time. Don't start in the middle of the book. Go through each step, whether you think you need it or not. If you skip a step, you could miss out on a vital ingredient to finding your everlasting love, even though some steps may not be as gratifying as others. It is the whole process that counts here, not one step or another. You certainly can't walk up a staircase by starting in the middle of it. Every step is as important as the first or last.

And maintain a positive attitude about your quest for everlasting love. This is not hard work; it is fun! You certainly want your love-life to be fun and not a chore, so your search for the right partner can be entertaining as well. Remember, the journey is just as important as the destination. If you come across an exercise that feels uncomfortable for you, it is just telling you that here is an area that needs more attention. But make it fun by challenging yourself to tackle the hard parts. You are your best motivator and you are the one who will benefit from the efforts you put into these exercises.

My guarantee to you is that, if you follow the instructions in this book, you will reach a new level of self-realization, become more focused on the type of partner you are seeking, achieve greater self-esteem, develop better communication skills, add more diversity to your life, and create a more interesting lifestyle. And, most importantly for so many single people, you will become all-around better at the dating game. Even couples who are seeking to renew their everlasting love vows have taken this program and created new ways of dating each other, as if they were beginning their romance for the first time. You will come out of the 12-step program with definite improvements in your persona, your outlook and the quality of your life.

The *12 Steps to Everlasting Love* is not an alternative to counseling or therapy, which may be needed for those who have serious, deep-seated problems in finding and maintaining a love relationship. However, this program can certainly enhance any counseling which the reader may be undergoing.

The *12 Steps to Everlasting Love* is not to be confused with the 12-step programs used in various organizations, most notably Alcoholics Anonymous (AA) which originated its 12-step plan over 50 years ago. While I value and appreciate the fine efforts of AA and other such groups, the *12 Steps to Everlasting Love* is an entirely different program designed to help you in your search for a lasting partnership.

This 30-Day Plan of Action is meant to help provide a structure for the development of your self-esteem and improvement in your social skills, both of which are critical to the success of finding and keeping everlasting love. I challenge you all to get out there and find even newer and better ways of meeting and mingling with each other. And I would love to hear stories from each of you about your progress.

"Fear grows out of the things we think; it lives in our minds. Compassion grows out of the things we are, and lives in our hearts."
Barbara Garrison

The Power of Everlasting Love

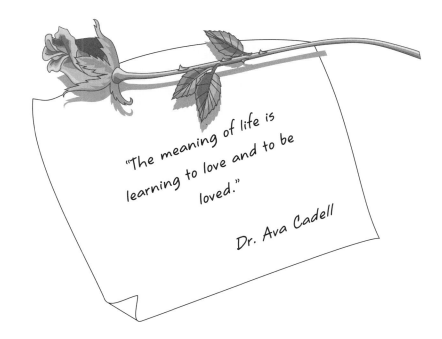

"The meaning of life is learning to love and to be loved."

Dr. Ava Cadell

The Power of Everlasting Love

Love is a give-give proposition, and everlasting love becomes 100% give on each side. The nature of love is to pour out, it wants to give. Love is being flexible. Couples who have achieved everlasting love don't tuck each other away in an ivory tower until it is convenient to be together. I know of one sad pair who only made love at 4 o'clock on Sunday afternoons because it suited one spouse's schedule. Do you think they stayed together? Eventually one began to play around on the other until it looked as though infidelity broke up their marriage. When two people are bound by everlasting love, they care enough to consider each other's needs and bend a little. To paraphrase a well-known allegory, the trees that can bow with the strongest breeze will survive any storm.

What love is not. Love is not handed to you on a silver platter. It is not automatic. If it were, it wouldn't be love. The very nature of love is that we grow into it. Love has a high value because it is an investment.

Love is not to be taken for granted. All too many couples give up trying when they have won each other; that's the very time to continue courting in new ways. Love is a precious gift that we earn, and anything we earn is all the more dear to us. You would not take a new car for granted; no, you keep up the maintenance for as long as the car lasts. Your everlasting love will need the same upkeep if you don't want to lose it.

Love is not a fleeting moment. It is not something you have one day and lose the next. We quest so for love because of its enduring quality and its ability to grow if nourished.

The ingredients of love. Like a good soup, love is made of many ingredients that blend just right. No one single element can serve as the whole meal. And it's hard to find a good soup recipe, isn't it? It needs special spices and maybe an unusual ingredient or two, like lotus root or exotic mushrooms. Even everyday potato soup has carrots, onions, garlic, salt; just the right seasonings.
Let's look at the ingredients in our love-potion soup. If you went to a sorcerer to help you find everlasting love, you would ask the magician to cook up the following:

Friendship. If you cannot rely on the person you love, then that person is not worthy of your love. And if your partner cannot count on you, you are not in everlasting love. Friendship means being able to say anything to your partner because you have that ease of "best buddies". Best friends never take advantage of each other; they are there to help one another. Any good partnership includes the same love you have for a best friend.

Trust. I am fond of an old — and trusted — axiom, that goes like this: "People who cannot trust should not be trusted". Distrusting people are often deceitful. I have found this to be a reliable measuring stick on the trust issue. But my rule-of-thumb is to give people the benefit of the doubt unless they prove otherwise. You cannot truly be connected to someone you cannot trust. That warm, mellow feeling we experience when we trust each other is a large part of everlasting love. Peace-of-mind in a relationship is vital to its stamina. And trust, like anything worthwhile, is something we earn over time, gradually.

Respect. As with trust, respect must be earned as well. It isn't automatic, although the seedlings of it may be there in the beginning of your relationship. Whether it can grow and blossom will determine the depth of your involvement. Respect can also diminish over time, and it is one of the most common reasons for ending a relationship. You must also respect yourself before someone else will respect you.

Passion. Yes, that all-consuming feeling of pure lust, euphoric, overwhelming, distracting, beautiful thing we call passion can be spontaneous or it can come on gradually, too. Passion either grows or it dissipates. Passion grows when you can be uninhibited with each other. And you break down any barriers by communicating. Passion fades when you have resentment, anger or contempt for your partner. Once again, here is an area that cannot be neglected or taken for granted in a relationship. Keep it alive by constantly creating new and exciting things to do together.

Communication. You cannot feel safe in a relationship without communication. You have to know where you stand, and you owe it to your partner to tell him or her the same. Knowing each other is the prerequisite to happiness in all areas. Communication is like that magic spice that brings out the flavor of all the other ingredients. Hey, that includes sex! Let your partner know it is safe to talk about fantasies and to explore them. Good communication can unleash strong creative energy between you and your partner. And with good communication, you can let your hair down and talk about anything. Not only does it enhance your partnership, it takes a big chunk out of everyday stress.

Growing with the power of love. Love heals. It can heal you, and it can heal your partner. Then the two of you together are like a new being, free to experience the present and future in all its possibilities, unhampered by the wounds of past relationships. Let's take a closer look at three domains of love.

Self love. The love of self is not conceit; conceit can be a lack of self-love or delusion about one's self in relation to others. I like what spiritual author Deepak Chopra says about love, because it fits into the meaning of loving and valuing one's self and self-worth: "You know that you have fully experienced love when you turn into love." You become love by first loving yourself. What we often don't realize is that no reason exists for not loving yourself. It ultimately doesn't matter what you were told as a child by others. You can work through your past and let go of it or you can hang on to it. But on your deathbed, it will be how much you have loved yourself and others that counts. Self-love issues account for crime, misery, poverty. No one should be without his or her own love. You are first your own best friend and your own support. You couldn't do anything without your own love and support to back you up. It pays to take your needs seriously. Do special things for yourself that you may have postponed until you are in a relationship. Buy yourself candy or special treats. Give yourself a bubble bath each day, go to the beach, rent classic movies, or get a massage. Get to know you and how to pamper you. Any love you experience beyond that will only be greater. You must love and care enough about yourself to begin healing your own wounds. Then the right partner can work together with you on bringing out more of your own love, just for you.

Loving your partner. When you have invested in you and in loving yourself more, you have that commodity to bring to a relationship. Loving your partner is ongoing. Everlasting love means continuing to demonstrate your affection and devotion from day one until the end of time. Show each other that love is the meaning of life. One young man, a college student named Bob, said to his girlfriend Anne: "You know I love you, you shouldn't have to be told." To the contrary, you and your partner cannot tell each other often enough how much you care for each other. It has taken Bob a few months to realize that love is about expression: saying it, showing it, acting it out. One of the best ways to communicate love is through giving emotional and appreciative compliments.

Loving each other. Everlasting love is a give-give relationship. And two givers have to be two receivers, also. If two "takers" enter a union, they will only drag each other down and beat each other up. And a "taker/giver" union won't last either. It may work for a while, but eventually the giver will run dry and resent not having his or her needs met as well. But two givers going into a relationship will have unity. They know the balance of giving and receiving. Take something as simple as giving a compliment. Compliments are vital in a relationship. It can make a world of difference in your day when your partner looks at you and says: "I desire you as much as the day I met you." And giving is an ongoing thing. For instance, it can be just as important to give each other trinkets, for no particular reason, than it is to lavish your partner on holidays, anniversaries or birthdays. People love to be surprised, especially with little things that mean so much. One friend of mine collects unusual rocks for a garden the way some people grow flowers. She loves it when her husband brings home a crystal or mineral for her collection, especially if he takes the time to learn something about it. Most important of all, giving of your time to each other has a priceless value on it. Our allotted time on this planet is so precious. And when that time runs out and we are ready to move on to the next dimension, it is the memories we have created here on earth that we will be thinking about. It is never too late to begin creating more loving memories with the people we care most about. At the end of your life, you won't be thinking about your bank account, the stock market, or business competition. But you will want to hold loving relationships and their memories close to you.

"Love is a canvas furnished by Nature and embroidered by imagination."

Voltaire

How to turn guilt into gilt:

Fairy tales often tell us about ancient sorcerers who would turn lead into gold. That's just what we want to do here. Guilt is like lead, isn't it? It weighs us down, it depresses us. And like the proverbial lead weight, it gives us a sinking feeling and holds us back like any excess baggage. Guilt has such a negative influence on people's lives. Guilt is leaden; it is toxic and can destroy the mind just like metallic lead can poison your body if you ingest it.

To turn guilt into gold, let's think of turning bad guilt into good guilt. One classic guilt situation is an ailing mother who makes her grown children feel guilty for not spending enough time with her. If her children dwell on their guilt, it will interfere with and destroy their entire lives. They will feel guilty for having fun with their own kids, or for going out to dinner with friends, or even for spending more time at work. To turn this situation around, this woman's children need to focus on the times they have spent with their mother, and stop dwelling on the times they cannot be with her. It will ease everyone's burden if this woman's offspring can dwell on all the things they have done for their mother, rather than dwelling on what they cannot do now.

Exercise:

Think of all the many different kinds of guilt and how you can alleviate your feelings of guilt. Here are a few sample subjects about which we all feel guilt: family, food, sex, relationships, religion, parents, work, health, money, infidelity, self-image, loving someone, hating someone, jealousy, procrastination. What are your own feelings about the areas of guilt in the exercises below?

Religious beliefs: Does my religion make me feel guilty about enjoying life? If so, how can I balance my spiritual life with my worldly life and feel okay?

Sexual guilt: Do I feel guilty about enjoying sex? Do I think sex is dirty, evil or unhealthy? Do I fear getting caught in the act? How can I remove these guilt barriers?

_____

_____

_____

_____

_____

_____

Procrastination: Do I feel so guilty about postponing what I have to do daily, that I end up procrastinating even more? How do I get out of this vicious cycle?

_____

_____

_____

_____

_____

_____

Another exercise in alleviating guilt is to write down everything that makes you feel guilty and what is causing the guilt feelings. I feel guilty about eating chocolate, which I love. And the guilt stems from a fear that my teeth will rot and that I will gain weight or my skin will break out in pimples. So I get rid of the guilt by eating chocolate in moderation. I allow myself one piece of chocolate a day and maybe two or three pieces over the weekend. By telling myself it's okay to eat some chocolate, the guilt goes away. And you know what? By getting rid of the guilt, I actually crave the chocolate less.

Turning guilt into gilt is indeed your golden challenge. The more you can get rid of excess-baggage guilt, the more you will be ready to find your everlasting love. Always look for the most pragmatic solution to any situation that causes you guilt. For instance, if you feel guilty about saying "no" to people, think of the unpleasant consequences of saying "yes" if you don't mean it. Also, try reversing your guilt patterns. If someone asks you to do a favor, don't say "okay" out of guilt. Stop the guilt feeling right then and there. You don't have to feel it. You can instead respond by saying "I'd like to help you out, but I can't because I'm very busy right now. I'm sure you understand."

Guilt is manageable. You don't have to go through life letting other people put their guilt on you; don't give them the satisfaction. Pity people who have to manipulate that way, but don't respond to them in kind. You can empower yourself more by showing love and sensitivity to the "guilt trippers" rather than letting them entrap you with their needs.

A large part of empowering yourself and your partner in a relationship is to open up about that old bugaboo guilt. Sometimes partners feel guilty when there's nothing to feel guilty about! And remember, anything can be negotiated. Let's say you feel guilty about not having enough sex with your mate. Then talk about it and work out a doable solution. The time you waste feeling guilty could be spent making spontaneous love!

"A smile is a light in the window of the soul indicating that the heart is home."

Anonymous

Dr. Ava's 12 Steps To Everlasting Love

The following 30-Day Plan of Action is a program to help you work through the 12 Steps to Everlasting Love in a structured fashion. Each of the four weeks relates to three of the twelve steps, with references to the prior steps as you progress through the 30 days.

Each week will have unique exercises as well as weekly review and reflection goals. Remember, there are no right or wrong answers to the questions. Use the following Emotion Barometers to guide you in expressing your feelings and thoughts as you complete the exercises and worksheets. The key to your success will be your honesty to yourself, your willingness to evaluate your answers, and your commitment to everlasting love.

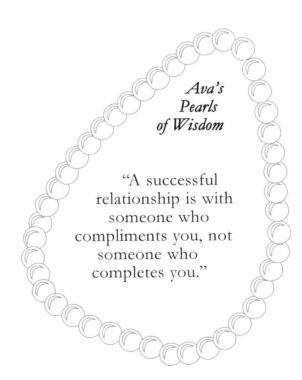

Ava's Pearls of Wisdom

"A successful relationship is with someone who compliments you, not someone who completes you."

WEEK ONE ~ HEALING

STEP 1: DEFINING EVERLASTING LOVE
"Once upon a time. . . . . . .and they lived happily ever after."

STEP 2: REVIEWING PAST RELATIONSHIPS
Assess what your past relationships had in common. Create closure.

STEP 3: BREAKING DOWN THE WALLS
Be willing to forgive and have the courage to trust again. Take risks.

WEEK TWO ~ VALUING YOURSELF

STEP 4: RAISING YOUR SELF-ESTEEM
By loving and accepting yourself, you will attract the right person.

STEP 5: APPRECIATING QUALITIES YOU BRING TO A RELATIONSHIP
Perceive all the positive elements of your personality and lifestyle.

STEP 6: DETERMINING THE QUALITIES YOU ARE LOOKING FOR
Prioritize and compile those qualities you are seeking in a partner.

WEEK THREE ~ FINDING EVERLASTING LOVE

STEP 7: FINDING YOUR EVERLASTING LOVE
Make the effort to analyze, explore and initiate meetings.

STEP 8: APPROACHING AND MAINTAINING COMMUNICATION
Conversation, like a relationship, involves both giving and taking.

STEP 9: EVALUATING YOUR DATING EXPECTATIONS
Avoid negative self-fulfilling prophecies. You will attract what you believe.

WEEK FOUR~ KEEPING EVERLASTING LOVE

STEP 10: MAKING YOUR PARTNER FEEL GOOD ABOUT HIM/HERSELF
Recognize your partner's attributes and incorporate them into words and actions.

STEP 11: LEARNING HOW TO FULFILL YOUR LOVER'S SEXUAL NEEDS
Learn your partner's needs, wants and desires through open communication.

STEP 12: COMMITTING YOURSELF TO EVERLASTING LOVE
Abide by the principles you have applied; sustain creativity, respect and support.

YOUR EMOTION BAROMETER

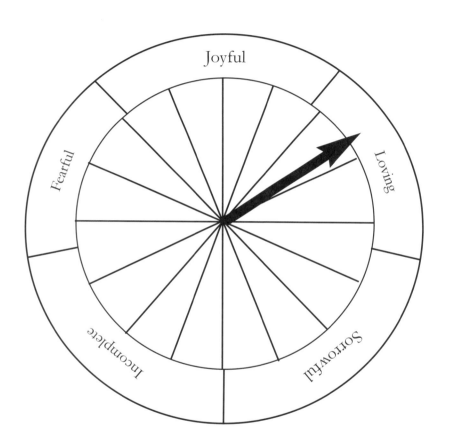

ba•rom•e•ter (beromiter) n. an instrument for measuring atmospheric pressures, used in forecasting weather and in estimating heights above sea level (*MERCURY BAROMETER, *ANEROID BAROMETER)
bar•o•mét•ric adjs
ba•rom•e•try n. the science of making barometric measurements

Use the following Emotion Barometers to guide you in expressing your feelings and thoughts as you complete the exercises and worksheets. The key to your success will be your honesty to yourself, your willingness to evaluate your answers, and your commitment to everlasting love.

YOUR EMOTION BAROMETER
Joyful

accepted
aglow
alive
amused
beautiful
brave
capable
cheerful
competent
confident
contented
courageous
curious
delighted
eager
ecstatic
elated
elevated
enthusiastic
euphoric
excited
exhilarated
fantastic

fine
free
fulfilled
glad
glowing
good
gratified
great
happy
high
hopeful
humorous
in high spirits
jazzed
jovial
light-hearted
loving
lustful
marvelous
neat
on cloud nine
on top of the world

optimistic
orgasmic
overjoyed
passionate
playful
pleasant
pleased
relieved
riding high
satisfied
sensational
sensual
serene
sexy
silly
strong
terrific
thankful
thrilled
turned on
up
witty
wonderful

YOUR EMOTION BAROMETER
Loving

admiration
adoration
affection for
affectionate
attached to
calm
captivated by
caring
cherish
close
comfortable
compassionate
concerned
desirable
devoted to
enamored
fond of
forgiving
friendly
generous
grateful

hold dear
hopeful
idolize
infatuated
like
lovable
loved
loyal
needed
passionate
peaceful
positive toward
prize
protective
proud
quiet
regard
relaxed
relieved
respected

respectful
safe
satisfied
secure
self-reliant
sentimental
special
supportive
sympathetic
taken with
tender
tenderness toward
trust
trusted
turned on
understanding
understood
valuable
warm
worship
worthwhile

YOUR EMOTION BAROMETER
Sorrowful

alienated
ashamed
awful
bad
barren
bashful
blah
bleak
blue
bored
defeated
dejected
demoralized
dependent
depressed
desolate
despair
devastated
disappointed
discouraged
dismal
distressed
downcast
embarrassed

empty
foolish
frustrated
gloomy
glum
grief
grim
hopeless
horrible
humiliated
hurt
ignored
in despair
isolated
lonely
lost
low
melancholy
miserable
nostalgic
pessimistic
regretful
rejected

remorseful
rotten
sad
shy
sorry
subdued
tearful
terrible
tired
troubled
unappreciated
unattractive
uncomfortable
uneasy
unfulfilled
unhappy
upset
uptight
vulnerable
weary
weepy
wishy-washy
worn-out
worried

YOUR EMOTION BAROMETER
Incomplete

anxious
apprehensive
ashamed
awkward
bewildered
confused
crippled
defeated
defensive
deficient
detached
emasculated
embarrassed
exasperated
finished
foolish
frantic
good for nothing
guilty
helpless
hopeless
humiliated
immobilized
impatient

impotent
inadequate
incapable
incompetent
indecisive
ineffective
inefficient
inept
inferior
inhibited
insecure
insignificant
intense
irritated
lacking
lacking confidence
like a failure
misunderstood
muddled
needy
neglected
no good
numb
overwhelmed

powerless
preoccupied
pressured
puzzled
rejected
restless
self-conscious
shaky
small
stubborn
stupid
touchy
ugly
unable
uncertain
unfit
unimportant
unsure of yourself
useless
vulnerable
washed up
weak
whipped
worthless

YOUR EMOTION BAROMETER
Fearful

afraid
alarmed
angry
annoyed
anxious
apprehensive
awkward
bashful
bitter
butterflies
claustrophobic
contemptuous
defensive
desperate
disgusted
distrustful
disturbed
doubtful
dread
edgy
embarrassed
envious

frightened
furious
hateful
hesitant
horrified
hostile
ill at ease
intimidated
irritable
jealous
jittery
jumpy
mean
nervous
on edge
pained
panicky
paralyzed
petrified
phony
prejudiced
pressured
provoked

resentful
risky
scared
self-conscious
shaky
shy
stage fright
tense
terrified
terror-stricken
threatened
tight
timid
trapped
uncomfortable
uneasy
unlovable
unsure
victimized
violated
vulnerable
worried

WEEK ONE
Healing

"Use your imagination
to create
romantic and lasting
memories."
Dr. Ava Cadell

Steps 1 through 3 are all about healing yourself.

There are two primary reasons why we don't find everlasting love. The single most important reason is attitude, negative attitude! How many times have you told yourself, "I'm never going to meet anyone special" or "I'm never going to fall in love"? With an attitude like that, you won't!

The second reason we don't find everlasting love is unrealistic expectation, not unlike the fairy tales we were raised to believe. Love has many stages, but many of us are frozen in the dewy-eyed, soft filter, Hollywood-romance stage. When the going gets tough, we bail out. Or, we don't even give love a chance because the person, timing or situation is not "perfect".

We have all been influenced by the behavior of our families, reinforced by our extra-familial life experiences. For example, if your parents always told you that they loved you but never showed it, their behavior would influence how you show your love to your partner today. If they told you they loved each other, but were constantly arguing and insulting one another, that, too, would influence how you communicate with your partner now. Of course, if you were raised in a loving environment—hugged and told every night that you were loved— that, too, would influence the way you love your partner.

The good news is that you don't have to be a prisoner of the way you were raised. You have the power to re-program yourself if you want to. And you can change your habits and attitudes that have been preventing you from finding your everlasting love. In all great journeys, the first step is the most critical and difficult, and this journey is no different. Congratulations, you have already taken the first step.

Now just open your eyes, step into the sunshine and enjoy the journey to everlasting love!

Instructions

Week One ~ HEALING
Step 1: Defining Everlasting Love
Step 2: Reviewing the Past
Step 3: Trusting Ag*ain*

Week One Instructions:

Steps 1-3

It is important to begin a daily routine that incorporates the philosophy and tenets of the 12 Steps to Everlasting Love. To keep your goals in mind, begin each day with a quick review of Dr. Ava's 12 Steps to Everlasting Love. The first week of your journey is devoted to mastering Steps 1-3.

Using the worksheet pages provided at the end of Week One, do the following on a daily basis:

♥ Stand in front of a full-length mirror naked. Write down which parts of your body you associate with sex. Which parts do you associate with displeasure and why? What would you like your body image to express to others? (e.g. healthy, sexy, sophisticated).

♥ Gaze at yourself from your feet to the top of your head. Pause at each part of your body. Don't move upward until you identify something positive, and record it on the daily worksheets. (Example: "My toes are perfectly shaped." or "I have a beautiful shape.")

♥ Write 3 affirmations before you start your day (Examples: "I am worthy of falling in love." or "I'm a great catch for someone.") Repeat these affirmations throughout the day (10 times each).

♥ Make a list of any compliments and/or criticisms you receive. Write down names of the individuals who gave them to you.

♥ Describe how you believe you are perceived by people with whom you come in daily contact. (Example: "I believe people think I'm intelligent and compassionate.")

♥ Review what you've written above and reflect on your interpersonal experiences of the day. Don't forget to include your emotions. Also reflect on any relationship experiences you may have observed in others from a distance, and how they affected you.

Using the worksheets provided at the end of Week One, do the following at least once during Week One:

♥ Choose one night this week, and every week thereafter, for your "personal entertainment." It is crucial that you discipline yourself and make time to socialize. Go out by yourself or with a friend. Go to a movie, dinner or for a walk to the park. Share your observations of others with your companion.

STEP 1
Defining Everlasting Love

"The story of a love is not important - what is important is that one is capable of love. It is perhaps the only glimpse we are permitted of eternity."

Helen Hayes

EXERCISES
STEP 1

Exercise #1: **Defining everlasting love.** Based on how you were raised, write down your definition of everlasting love. There are no right or wrong answers, but it is quite valuable to articulate your concept of everlasting love since more often than not, consciously or unconsciously, this is the standard by which we measure our relationships. For example, "One day I will meet my soul mate. We will have no conflicts, and we will never have to work at our relationship."

_____

_____

_____

_____

Exercise #2: **Family behavior.** How has your family's behavior influenced you? In other words, in your home life, what behavior did you observe and then adopt as your own? Examples: Your father or brother was a womanizer. Your parents said they loved you but weren't affectionate. Your parents claimed to be happy but they didn't act it. One parent dominated the family. How did these influences affect your picture of love?

_____

_____

_____

_____

Exercise #3: **Attitudes.** What negative attitudes do you have in regard to finding true love? Most of us have a self-fulfilling, doomsday attitude about love and romance. If you can tell yourself the truth about how you imagine finding long-term love, you can influence the result. For example, "I'm afraid that everlasting love won't last because my partner may stray and leave me for someone else."

_____

_____

_____

_____

Exercise #4: List and prioritize what is most important to you in your life (e.g. work, family, money, health, fun, friends, spirituality, etc.).

_____

_____

_____

Exercise #5: List three things that make you happy.

_____

_____

Exercise #6: List three things that make you unhappy.

_____

_____

Exercise #7: Write down the names of people who influenced your life positively, and explain how they did so.

_____

_____

_____

Exercise #8: Make a list of those people who have hurt you, when and how.

_____

_____

_____

_____

Exercise #9: List how you see yourself (e.g. strong, cute, insecure, friendly, healthy, lonely, etc.).

_____

_____

_____

_____

Exercise #10: List how you think other people perceive you (e.g. attractive, intelligent, successful, arrogant, etc.).

_____

_____

_____

_____

"Love can all
but raise the dead."
Emily Dickinson

STEP 2
Reviewing Past Relationships

"Better to have loved and lost, than to have never loved at all."

St. Augustine

Step 2: Reviewing the Past

As you reflect on your relationships, it is important to value the lessons you have learned. Every situation that crosses our path is a gift, but not all gifts come with cheerful packaging. It is how we perceive the gift and what we do with it that counts. So, unless you examine everything that happens to you, and ask yourself, "What have I learned from this?" a precious gift might just pass you by.

Step 2 includes:

1. Listing how many love relationships you've had.
2. Evaluating the pluses and minuses of each association.
3. Looking for repetitive patterns.
4. Creating and accepting closure.

The fact that a relationship ends does not mean it's a failure. I believe it lasts just as long as it was intended to, long enough for you to learn whatever you needed and then move on.

In this second step, I'd like you to concentrate on past relationships and focus on the reasons why you think they ended. Do you notice any patterns like the following: You always left them or perhaps they always left you. Maybe they were all relationships based on physical attraction and they lacked substance. Perhaps they ended because of power struggles or just a lack of compatibility. Maybe all your relationships came to a halt when love became tied in with commitment. It doesn't matter whose fault it was. What matters is to see the patterns at play and to create closure.

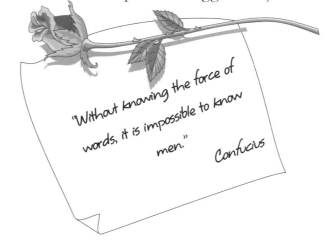

"Without knowing the force of words, it is impossible to know men."

Confucius

Rejection

"An act of love that fails is just as much a part of the divine life as an act of love that succeeds, for love is measured by fullness, not by reception."
Harold Loukes

What Rejection Is:

Rejection is a feeling we generate within ourselves when our targeted prospect appears to rebuff us.   But always remember, it is the situation that is being turned down, not necessarily you. A famous Hollywood actress once joked about the many rejections she received before achieving her ultimate success. Of the various roles for which she auditioned, she was, she laughed, too fat, too thin, too short, too tall, too glamorous, too plain, and on and on. In other words, she learned that rejection is temporary and situational. In fact, this actress, who is a very pretty woman, also admitted to having been rejected numerous times by the opposite sex. So you see, everyone on this planet has been rejected by someone, somewhere at some time or other. In a vast, ever-moving sea of five billion people, your quota of rejection may actually be smaller than you think.

According to a couple of Webster's many definitions of rejection, the word can simply mean to refuse to take, to decline. Do you suppose flowers feel rejected if you don't pick them? No, they can bask in their beauty whether anyone picks them or not. Do animals at the pet store feel rejected if you are unable to give them a good home? Who knows? But your rejection of the pet does not mean it is an unworthy animal. And most likely, the little animal will attract the right home despite many rejections. Let's take this definition game a bit further. If we look up rejection in Roget's Thesaurus, we find corresponding terms like setback and reverse. These are not quite so scary as a downright refusal. Setbacks are only delays, and reverse just means to turn around and keep going until you find the right direction.

Curiously, rejection can be one of your guardian angels. Rejection may be an indicator of the wrong timing, the wrong pathway, or the wrong situation for you. Rejection may be fate barring you from an even worse experience than being turned down. Rejection may mean that you've been spared a limited partnership with someone who is not quite on your wavelength. Or rejection can be nature's way of telling you to reassess who you are and what you want.

Rejection is a feeling of powerlessness that can make you falsely feel you are not in control. Someone turned you down; the final decision was in their hands. But you are in control — that is the key. As an adult, you have the power to let rejection work for you, not against you. When you feel rejected, it is nature's way of telling you to take the power back. Rejection is just a stepping stone to get you from one side of the river to the other, or shall we say, one goal at a time. Rejection can be momentary. The situation may change, or the targeted date may change his/her mind at another time. Rejection is just a healthy signal to move on, for the moment.

What Rejection Is Not:

Rejection is not failure. But a rejection can make you feel like you have failed. It is necessary for us to conquer this feeling of failure. Otherwise, a simple turn-down can be blown out of proportion to reality. The sense of failure you experience may be telling you that you are taking on too much responsibility for the situation. Many reasons exist as to why another person may say no, and those reasons are rarely a personal attack on you. Stop and think twice before you let other people's cold-shoulders cause you to feel like an unacceptable human specimen. You don't know what is going on in their lives. They may already be attached, they may have health or financial problems, they could be moving to another state, they may be afraid of being hurt, they may be unhappy with their job, or their dog could have just died.

Rejection is not a total loss, even though it feels that way at first. We just met the one person who we think is everything we have been looking to find...and, to our absolute shock and dismay, that person has the temerity to turn us down. Will we ever meet anyone like this again? In a world of millions of single people, the possibilities of whom you can meet defy imagination, especially as the world grows much smaller through computers and more social mobility.

In fact, this temporary feeling of loss we experience when we are rejected is a grieving for the intimacy we hoped we had, at last, found. And it slipped through our fingertips by a single, "No." We think to ourselves, "What did we do wrong? What did we say wrong? Why doesn't the other person see our compatibility with him or her?" While it can be helpful to analyze your appearance or your approach, don't sweat the small stuff. You met someone in a fleeting moment; it was simply an opportunity that didn't come to pass. You never lost what you never had. The person or situation simply may not be as compatible as you first thought it to be. And, the fish that got away makes room for a whole new school of fish that will swim in your direction.

How to Move Beyond Rejection:

Practice makes perfect. What you can glean from rejection, can give you a confidence unlike any you have ever experienced. How you handle the rejection can be a powerful exercise in mastering any runaway emotions that get stirred up within you. Do you feel worthless after being rejected?   If so, how could you take charge over your feelings and handle the situation differently?   A middle-aged woman named Jessica was once painfully rejected by a man who had had a bad day, and he chose her to "dump on." Jessica felt like a discarded rag afterward. Challenging herself to just come out ahead, she wrote the man a letter expressing her regret at their miscommunication and the poor timing. She laid out her intentions and honest motives. Jessica also pointed out that his unkind, exaggerated viewpoint of her was not quite true. The letter had a calm, non-threatening, easygoing tone. She did not even expect a response. "I wrote him the letter just to end the situation on a positive note," she said. The man called her right after he got the letter and apologized, expressing more civil behavior and a great appreciation for Jessica's thoughtful letter to him.

If the pain of any rejection is stronger than it should be for the experience, then bring all the pain up and work it out of your system.   Don't be afraid to feel old wounds.   Go off by yourself, or go to a close friend or relative, and let the ill pain overwhelm you until you can clearly see what that pain is trying to tell you.   Emotional pain can be an ally if you let it "talk" to you.

Working through outworn feelings is more comfortable in the long run than carrying confusing old wounds around within you. If you have a cut on your hand, you can do one of three things: 1) Leave it alone, and it will heal on its own; 2) Care for the injury with ointment and bandages, and it will heal faster, or 3) Pick at the wound, and it will never heal. Emotional wounds are no different. Harboring and picking at those old, stale hurts just keeps them recycling through your system where they eventually manifest as illness. What's more, they can send a red flag to other people that you feel rejected, even when you truly accept yourself and all you are. Once you've expunged a deep-seated emotional wound or misplaced sentiment, then reward yourself by moving on to the next prospect. After a while, rejection may become a motivator, not a deterrent to your progress in everlasting love.

"If you judge someone, you have no time to love them."
Mother Teresa

EXERCISES
STEP 2

Exercise #1: **Relationships.** List your most significant love relationships of the past, with the positive and negative aspects of each. For example, "Sex was good, communication was poor, we were incompatible."

_____

_____

_____

_____

_____

_____

Exercise #2: **Endings.** Reflect on these past relationships and list the reasons (you think) they did not work out. For example, "My last relationship ended because it simply lacked passion, common values or open communication."

_____

_____

_____

_____

Exercise #3: **Patterns.** Look for repetitive patterns, both positive and negative. Can you see how these patterns bear a resemblance to your family's relationship problems? List notable patterns, both good and bad. For example, "All my relationships were based on sex, all my partners were abusive or selfish."

_____

_____

_____

_____

Exercise #4: **Changes.** What do you think would have been different in your relationships if you had changed? Finish the following sentence with as many endings as you can.

If only I had _____

_____

_____

_____

_____

Now eliminate all the above statements that you have no control over such as you race, gender, religion, size and such. Stop punishing yourself and rid yourself of all guilt and shame. It's time to move on.

Exercise #5: **Closure.** Choose one relationship that still needs closure. Then, write in the space below what you might say to the other person in this incomplete relationship, if he or she were with you right now. And what would you like that person to communicate back to you? (This is about forgiveness, incompleteness, cleaning up lies, etc.) For example, "I'm sorry that our relationship ended without my communicating my physical needs and desires to you. I should have been more open and honest with you." And you might want the other person to say, "It's OK. We had good times. We had bad times. I choose to remember the good times."

_____

_____

_____

Exercise #6: **Happiness.** At what time and place in your life were you the happiest?

_____

_____

_____

_____

_____

Exercise #7: **More Happiness.** Who was with you when you felt the happiest?

_____

_____

_____

_____

_____

_____

Exercise #8: **Accomplishments.** Write down all of the accomplishments you have made in the last year. For example, "I have lost five pounds, I can say 'no' more easily, I work out regularly, or I got a raise at work." Now choose which accomplishments were most satisfying to you and highlight them.

_____

_____

_____

_____

_____

_____

_____

_____

_____

_____

_____

_____

_____

_____

STEP 3
Breaking Down The Walls

"Love cures people, both the ones who give it and the ones who receive it."

Dr. Karl Menninger

Step 3: Breaking Down the Walls - Trusting Again

It's so hard to trust once we've been hurt. We put up our defenses and close our hearts. Yet, we still expect to find everlasting love. The fact is if you can't trust then you can't expect people to trust you either. It's a vicious cycle, and until you're willing to forgive yourself and others for the hurt you feel, you will not be ready for everlasting love.

Self-forgiveness means getting the old, stale hurts and emotional confusions out of our way. That may involve grieving for what didn't work out or grieving because we have to relinquish situations that are not entirely in our best interest. Most of all, self-forgiveness means picking up those emotional roadblocks and moving them off the relationship highway. These hindrances serve only to impede our progress towards our goals.

Forgiving others means letting go of your hurt and anger so that both of you can move on and grow somewhere else. It can be scary to admit the power our old wounds hold over us. Resentments seemingly protect the hurting heart. However, forgiveness is a form of unburdening, removing emotional clutter that can prevent you from experiencing everlasting love. Once we realize all that we're missing, forgiveness becomes a much welcome relief. Forgiveness can lead to emotional freedom, which can lead to change. And that's good because it is your life you want to change. Forgiveness is about uncovering hurts rather than denying they are there. Forgive others for the pain they have inflicted upon you, and forgive yourself for allowing it.

Need help learning how to forgive? Try writing a letter to the person who hurt you (including yourself!) and don't forget to say, "I forgive you" at the end. You could also create your own forgiveness tape. Say the words that allow you to let go of your hurt. Make a personal affirmation, and repeat it to yourself when you feel the hurt sneaking up on you. Fearlessly examine what keeps you trapped in being unforgiving. What's the payoff? What are the reasons for not forgiving? We can be reluctant to forgive because it might make us feel weak, we may lose our power in the relationship, we may feel taken advantage of, we may be afraid, or we may want to hold on to the hatred. However, cataloging your resentments keeps you from experiencing the love you want.

Relationships are created because of attraction, and unlike the laws of physics, the law of attraction dictates that like attracts like. What do I mean by this? If you have low self-esteem, you are letting someone know that you don't think much of yourself, which means you're potentially setting yourself up for failure. We attract the person we think we're worthy of. If you've been hurt and wounded--and if you don't heal that wound--you will attract someone similar to you. Negative attracts negative, positive attracts positive.

The healing process takes time. I'm not suggesting you jump right into another relationship immediately. But I am encouraging you to give new people the benefit of the doubt because they haven't hurt you. This is the time to take risks. If you don't do anything different then nothing different will happen to you. You must forgive before you can move on.

"You are the one you
are looking for."

Audre Lourde

Forgiveness

"One word frees us of all the weight and pain in life. That word is love."

Sophocles

What forgiveness is:

Forgiveness is for giving to yourself. It is a gift for you on your pathway to everlasting love, one that can help you clear up emotional wounds which may be hampering your success in finding and holding the right partner. Forgiveness means to free up those hurts inside you. Then you can breathe that clear, heady, elevated air of emotional freedom. And that's when you become open to the partner who is truly right for you. Without mistakes, there can be no forgiveness; without forgiveness, there can be no love. As a popular spiritual teacher puts it, "forgiveness is necessary in igniting the spark of love".

Forgiveness is release. The word "forgive" literally means "to give up", "to give away". Forgiveness is a form of unburdening, removing emotional clutter that can keep you blocked from experiencing everlasting love. Forgiveness can lead to emotional freedom and that can lead to change. And it is your life that you want to change. Forgiveness is about uncovering hurts rather than denying they are there. Forgiveness has to do with acknowledging all those creepy crawly feelings that block you from your joy.

One simple exercise is to forgive yourself each week for the mistakes you made. Set aside a few minutes to review what went wrong, and how you might better have handled the situation. A client of mine, Jane, has learned to stop wasting her time blaming others for what they have done to her. Instead, she opens up her weekly forgiveness ritual with something like this: "I forgive myself for going out on a blind date and expecting love-at-first-sight," or "I forgive myself for putting up with a man who belittled me." By forgiving herself in this manner, she remains focused on her needs rather than what is lacking in the other person. As Jane says: "When I release my resentments this way each week, it clears me up inside. I don't hear that rumble of anger underneath my breath anymore. And it helps me to stay focused on me and my expectations."

Forgiveness is for giving to yourself what you didn't get enough of as a child: attention, love, affection, recognition and more. We all missed out on something. Whoever or whatever denied you your needs in the past can be forgiven — released — to make more room for what you want to experience in a relationship. Draw yourself out; don't wait for others to do it for you. Allow them the pleasure of knowing you better. Reward yourself by becoming the center of attention at a party; don't be afraid to stand out. Notice how other people will love you if you allow them. If you have a pet, take note of how that animal loves just being around you. Permit other people to enjoy your company in the same way; let yourself be flattered by their attention. Pamper yourself with the affections of others. If you hug almost any human being, they will generally hug you back. And that one little hug per day can prove that the love you have to give is very, very worthy.

Forgiveness is daring to feel worthy of the love you seek, giving up what you may have accepted as love in the past, especially if it was wrong for you. Forgiveness is having the courage to confront a two-fold roadblock: self-forgiveness and for giving-up the limitations of others.

What forgiveness is not:

A relationship ends when it needs to end. If the union was a mistake, that only means it was a growing experience. It's okay to make relationship mistakes, as long as you don't keep repeating them. And in your next relationship, you'll make new mistakes; that's what growing is all about.

Forgiveness is not a quickie emotion which magically lets you "forgive and forget". You know, it is more essential to forgive than to forget. Forgiveness is getting the venom out of your system so you won't carry the festering snake bite into your next relationship. But we don't want to completely forget those poisons and irritants we have extracted from our failed marriages, friendships, and partnerships. We have earned the right to retain the memories of our blackest, ugliest relationship experiences and turn them into shiny, attractive "black pearls". These hard-earned "black pearls" of garnered insight and wisdom will keep us from making the same mistakes over and over. And, as you may know, a black pearl is more rare and more priceless on the market than a white pearl. Or, shall we say, experience can be our best teacher?

It can be scary to admit the power our old wounds hold over us. They can go back decades in time. Once we realize, re-feel, our old wounds to the point of boredom, forgiveness becomes a much welcome relief. This is especially so when we realize what we are missing out there in the world. Rather than building up more resentment because we are "supposed to" forgive, real forgiveness (cleansing the hurt feelings, misinterpretations and misunderstandings) can become as simple as taking the emotional trash out of our lives.

How to move beyond forgiveness:

Forgiveness is two-fold, self-forgiveness and forgiving others. Self-forgiveness means getting the old, stale hurts and emotional confusions out of our way. That may involve grieving for what didn't work out, or grieving because we have to relinquish situations that are not for our highest good. Most of all, self-forgiveness is to pick up those emotional roadblocks and move them off the relationship highway; these hindrances don't belong there. And forgiving others means to get their emotional junk out of your life, so both you and they can move on and grow somewhere else.

Forgive yourself for thinking that you cannot find everlasting love, for any ridiculous reason. To forgive the self is to stop the cycle of self-punishment long enough to look down better avenues that can lead to everlasting love. This will mean bringing up deep, suppressed emotions from time to time, but you will not be alone.

Below are a few simple, but effective, steps to help you clear the decks and move on. Perhaps you would like to share them with a friend or even a new love interest.

1. **Forgive for the sake of it.** Refusing to forgive can hurt you more than it hurts the other person. Why should you carry the burden?

2. **Give up the grievance right away.** You wouldn't hold a grudge against an aged, infirm person who unintentionally offended you. You might even view that person with pity. So why not discount everyone who offends you? Don't waste your valuable energy dwelling on the wrongs done to you. Other people don't always know what they are doing; sometimes they can't even help themselves. By making light of whomever is causing you grief, you are giving them less power to hurt you.

3. **Put the spiritual love potion to work.** Bad thoughts about others just fuel the hatred, and that gets you nowhere. Good thoughts make up the love potion that will heal you and may even give you a healthier outlook on your old relationships, creating a more loving state of mind. Bad thoughts are like hamsters running backward on a Ferris wheel. A good thought is like a bird flying freely in the sky--productive. Remember, other people have been hurt, too. We often don't keep that in mind when dealing with each other during our busy days. But every person on this planet has been hurt, sometimes over and over again. A friend of mine, Keith, puts it this way: "I'll bet if I were to tell you about all the times people have hurt me, you'd prefer your own hurts and troubles to mine," he jokes. "The grass isn't any greener in my backyard. I just don't let life's pains get me down." Keith simply doesn't let hurt feelings bother him for any length of time.

4. **Unload your backpack.** Get rid of your hatred and "hurtreds" before they congeal and petrify. Unload your emotional backpack; don't let it weigh you down and impede your quest for everlasting love. Talk to yourself in the mirror, talk to friends, a counselor, an empty chair, a stuffed animal, a movie star's photo or even a pet.   Just get the old emotions out in the open. Or write a letter to the person who harmed you. Bravely detail the situation clearly and calmly, without anger. Then you can rise above and beyond the pains with a healthy sense of power over your emotions. And always say "I forgive you" at the end because life is too short to live it in hostility.   Forgive others for the behavior they inflicted upon you, and forgive yourself for allowing it.

5. **Forgive yourself and others freely; don't hold back.** Create your own special forgiveness tape or affirmation. Say or write words that allow you to deeply let go of what is hurting you about the other person's behavior. Don't hold anything back. Make it unconditional. Then let the situation go.

6.   **Look inside yourself.** Take the brave quantum leap and fearlessly examine what keeps you trapped in being unforgiving. What's the payoff? What are the reasons for not forgiving? We can be reluctant to forgive because it might make us feel weak, we may lose our power in the relationship, we may feel taken advantage of, we may be afraid or we may want to hold on to the hatred, just wishing people would die. Heaven forbid, but is it possible that cataloging your resentments is keeping you from experiencing the love you want? Real power in a relationship comes with clearing the blockages and creating more room for everlasting love. It takes strength to forgive; running away from forgiveness is weak. The other person will not take advantage of your forgiving nature if both of you sincerely want a relationship to grow. You won't lose control by forgiving; in fact, your relationships can become more manageable by forgiving and working things out. And we all know that love and fear are like oil and water; they never mix. Love is strength; fear is weakness. Forgiving is a very bold act of confident love, and confidence in yourself. And love is real power that can be everlasting.

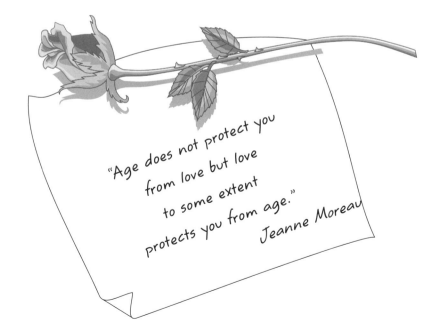

"Age does not protect you from love but love to some extent protects you from age."

Jeanne Moreau

EXERCISES
STEP 3

We all too often generalize about the opposite sex. Consequently we expect the other gender to disappoint us, and when we expect something to happen, it usually does. Let's get rid of the many misconceptions. Conceive it, believe it and you will achieve it.

Exercise #1: **The opposite sex.** What are your beliefs about the opposite sex? Fill in these blanks.

Men/Women always

_____

_____

_____

Men/Women never

_____

_____

_____

I wish Men/Women would

_____

_____

_____

Exercise #2: **Guilt.** Write down three things that you currently feel guilty about.

_____

_____

_____

_____

Exercise #3: **Forgiveness.** What habits or patterns from the past would you like to abandon moving forward? Write three affirmations. For example, if you feel that you couldn't keep your commitments in past relationships, your affirmation might be: "I am a very committed person now. I love committed relationships. I thrive on commitment." It's okay to feel guilt as long as you move on and forgive yourself.

Affirmation #1:
_____
_____

Affirmation #2:
_____
_____
_____

Affirmation #3:
_____
_____
_____

Exercise #4: List three people you need to forgive and why you need to forgive them.

I forgive _____ for _____

I forgive _____ for _____

I forgive _____ for _____

Exercise #5: **Trust.** People who can't trust, are (almost) always not trustworthy themselves. Write down the greatest fears you have when it comes to trust. For example: Abandonment, being taken advantage of, being manipulated, being abused.

_____
_____

Who and what do you trust? (Your father, mother, yourself, your faith, that you'll keep your job, etc.)

_____

_____

_____

_____

_____

_____

Exercise #6: **Risk.** List the kinds of risks that you know you have to take in order to have the kind of life you really want. How willing are you to take these risks? (For example: Smile at strangers, talk to people you don't know, try a new activity, go to a place you haven't dared go before, wear something out of character.)

_____

_____

_____

_____

_____

Exercise #7: **Priorities.** List your top 4 priorities in order to find Everlasting Love. (eg: Go out more often, take a class, initiate conversations, etc.)

_____

_____

_____

_____

_____

_____

Worksheet Week One ~ Monday:

These are the positive things I noted about myself in my morning look in the mirror:

_____

_____

_____

These are the things I am grateful for today:

_____

_____

_____

_____

Write three affirmations everyday and say them to myself at least ten times. Example, "I am worthy of falling in love."

_____

_____

_____

_____

_____

Make a list of any compliments and criticisms I've received today, and the people who said them.

Compliments: _____

_____

_____

Criticisms: _____

_____

_____

People I smiled at or complimented today:

_____

Where I spent my social time and what I observed:

_____

_____

My only regret today was:

_____

_____

What I've learned today:

_____

_____

_____

How does it make me feel?

_____

_____

*Ava's
Pearls
of Wisdom*

"If you keep
doing what you've
always done, you'll
keep getting what
you've always gotten."

Worksheet Week One ~ Tuesday:

These are the positive things I noted about myself in my morning look in the mirror:

_____
_____
_____

These are the things I am grateful for today:

_____
_____
_____

These are the things that disappointed me today:

_____
_____
_____

Repeat yesterday's affirmations, write one new one today. Say them at least ten times. Example, "I am worthy of happiness."

_____
_____

Make a list of any compliments and criticisms I've received today, and the people who said them.

Compliments:

_____
_____

Criticisms:

_____
_____

People I smiled at or complimented today:

_____
_____
_____

Where I spent my social time and what I observed:

_____

_____

The funniest thing that happened today was:

_____

_____

_____

My biggest obstacle today was:

_____

_____

What I've learned today:

_____

_____

_____

Use the following space for additional notes.

Ava's
Pearls
of Wisdom

"Many people
give up just when
they are about
to achieve success."

Worksheet Week One ~ Wednesday:

These are the positive things I noted about myself in my morning look in the mirror:

_____

_____

_____

These are the things I am grateful for today:

_____

_____

_____

Write one more affirmation today and say it to myself at least ten times. Example, "I am worthy of being healthy." Repeat the affirmations from Monday and Tuesday.

_____

_____

Make a list of any compliments and criticisms I've received today, and the people who said them.

Compliments:

_____

_____

Criticisms:

_____

_____

List some negative thoughts that I would like to banish from my life (e.g. too fat, sensitive, suspicious):

_____

People I smiled at or complimented today:

_____

_____

Where I spent my social time and what I observed:

_____

_____

My favorite time of day was: because:

_____

_____

_____

_____

The following emotions best describe my day today (use the emotional barometer):

_____

_____

What I've learned today:

_____

_____

_____

Use the following space for additional notes.

**Ava's
Pearls
of Wisdom**

"It's never too late
to improve yourself."

Worksheet Week One ~ Thursday:

These are the positive things I noted about myself in my morning look in the mirror:

_____

_____

_____

These are the things I am grateful for today:

_____

_____

_____

_____

Write another affirmation today and say it to myself at least ten times. Example, "I am worthy of the best in life." Add to daily affirmations from earlier this week. Continue repeating them daily.

_____

_____

Make a list of any compliments and criticisms I've received today, and the people who said them.

Compliments:

_____

_____

Criticisms:

_____

_____

People I smiled at or complimented today:

_____

_____

Where I spent my social time and what I observed:

_____

_____

Today I wish I had more:

_____

_____

Today I wish I had less:

_____

_____

I felt powerful when:

_____

_____

What I've learned today:

_____

_____

Use the following space for additional notes.

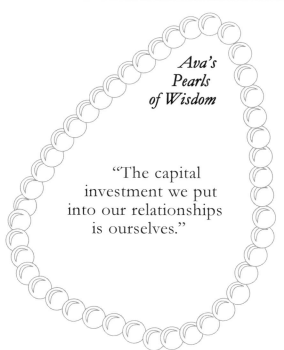

*Ava's
Pearls
of Wisdom*

"The capital
investment we put
into our relationships
is ourselves."

Worksheet Week One ~ Friday:

These are the positive things I noted about myself in my morning look in the mirror:

_____

_____

_____

These are the things I am grateful for today:

_____

_____

_____

Write one more affirmation today. Say all to myself from the week so far at least ten times. Example, "I am worthy of fulfillment in my career."

_____

_____

Make a list of any compliments and criticisms I've received today, and the people who said them.
Compliments:

_____

_____

Criticisms:

_____

_____

People I smiled at or complimented today:

_____

_____

Where I spent my social time and what I observed:

_____

_____

_____

If I could erase one thing from today, it would be:

_____

_____

_____

What was the best thing that happened to me today?

_____

_____

_____

I was most comfortable today when:

_____

What I've learned today:

_____

_____

_____

Use the following space for additional notes.

Ava's Pearls of Wisdom

"Whatever you love to do, you will do well."

Worksheet Week One ~ Saturday:

These are the positive things I noted about myself in my morning look in the mirror:

_____

_____

_____

These are the things I am grateful for today:

_____

_____

Repeat the week's affirmations and add a new one for today. Say all of them at least ten times. Today's affirmation might be: "I am worthy of having everlasting love ."

_____

_____

Make a list of any compliments and criticisms I've received today, and the people who said them.
Compliments:

_____

Criticisms:

_____

_____

People I smiled at or complimented today:

_____

Where I spent my social time and what I observed:

_____

_____

_____

How did I express myself today? (e.g. Outgoing, frustrated, confident)

_____

_____

_____

_____

_____

The person that most influenced me today was: because:

_____

_____

_____

What I've learned today:

_____

_____

_____

Use the following space for additional notes.

Ava's
Pearls of
Wisdom

"Enthusiasm and
success just seem to
go together."

Worksheet Week One ~ Sunday:

As Week One comes to a close, these are the positive things I noted about myself in my morning look in the mirror:

_____

_____

_____

These are the things I am grateful for today:

_____

_____

_____

Add a new affirmation to those of the previous week and say them to myself at least ten times. Example for today, "I am worthy of being a success in life and love."

_____

_____

Make a list of any compliments and criticisms I've received today, and the people who said them.
Compliments:

_____

_____

Criticisms:

_____

_____

People I smiled at or complimented today:

_____

_____

Where I spent my social time and what I observed:

_____

_____

_____

What I've learned today:

_____

_____

_____

The person I would have liked to spend more time with was:

_____

_____

The person I saw today who was most like me was:

_____

_____

Use the following space for additional notes.

Ava's
Pearls
of Wisdom

"A loving, faithful
partner is the
greatest treasure."

At the End of Week One:
Preview Steps 4, 5 and 6, and review steps 1-3, before you begin Week Two.
The first week of the 12 Steps to Everlasting Love is dedicated to healing. Week 2 is focused
on self- value. Once we have begun healing the wounds and patterns of the past, then we can focus on
appreciating who we really are and what we bring to a relationship. As much as possible, incorporate more of the outside
world into your program. Share what develops in Steps 4-6 with people close to you.

WEEK TWO

Valuing Yourself

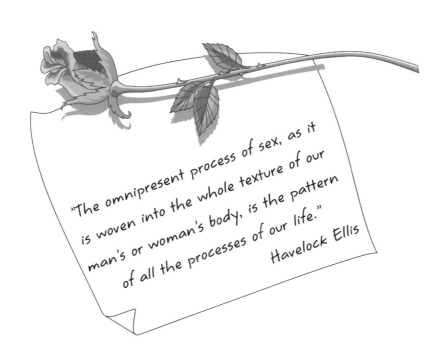

"The omnipresent process of sex, as it is woven into the whole texture of our man's or woman's body, is the pattern of all the processes of our life."

Havelock Ellis

Steps 4 through 6 are all about self-value.

When you're kind to yourself, you project that kindness to others. After all, you catch more flies with honey than with vinegar. When you're filled with negative energy, obviously you are going to attract negative people.

Begin by loving yourself and accepting yourself just the way you are with all your idiosyncrasies (and we all have them). Accept your weaknesses, your strengths, your guilt and insecurities as part of your make-up.

This is the time to pamper yourself, to prove how valuable you are and to take the time to do something special for yourself. Maybe you have always wanted to stay at a beachfront hotel, get a massage or a pedicure, learn a new language, rent a particular movie, or have a gourmet dinner served in your home. No matter how big or small, the time to fulfill your desires is now.

Whatever it is, make a commitment to honor and love yourself. For example, "I promise to pamper myself with a warm bubble bath at least once a week." If you can't pamper yourself, then you can't expect anyone else to do so.

"Without mistakes, there is no forgiveness; without forgiveness, there is no love."

Dr. Ava Cadell

Instructions

Week Two ~ VALUING YOURSELF

Step 4: Raising Your Self-Esteem
Step 5: Qualities You Bring To A Relationship
Step 6: Determining The Qualities You're Looking For

Week Two Instructions:

Steps 4-6

It is important to proceed with this 30-Day Plan-of-Action at a pace that feels comfortable. However, you must keep moving forward in your program, keeping focused on the ultimate goal. Don't allow a temporary setback or minor negativism in an encounter to dissuade you. In the first week, you learned to confront past relationships objectively. Being aware of obstacles from your past is important. Learn to observe before you react to any situation.

Using the worksheet pages provided at the end of Week Two, do the following on a daily basis:

♥ Continue to do your mirror work. But now, instead of concentrating on your body, focus on your eyes. Look deeply into your eyes for three to five minutes daily, thinking to yourself (or saying aloud) "I love you."

♥ Continue to write your three affirmations at the start of each day. Concentrate on qualities. (Examples: "I am a really caring person" or "I make people feel good about themselves"). Repeat these affirmations to yourself throughout the day (10 times each).

♥ Write down two more fun things that you would like to do, and add these to the list from Week One. Schedule at least one, if not two, of these activities before Week Two is over. To the greatest extent possible, combine these activities with your goal of expanding your social circle.

♥ Notice attractive behavior in someone of the opposite sex and evaluate it, adding it to a list of attributes for your everlasting love (e.g. easy going, intelligent, happy, etc.). Assign priorities to these qualities.

♥ When you notice attractive behavior in a member of your own sex, incorporate that trait into your own style (e.g. new hair style, different clothing, weight loss, new attitude, new level of maturity, spiritual interests, etc.). Consider ways to improve your own self-image (Steps 4 and 5).

♥ Extend a friendly greeting as well as a smile to two or more people every day.

♥ Continue to spend time each day (away from home or work) where you are able to observe social interaction among others. It is imperative now that you begin to include others in your social activities. Increase your sphere of friends. Invite someone special to share your social time. Share your observations, feelings and reactions.

♥ List three more positive things you can bring to a relationship.

♥ End each day with a review of your lists, observations and interactions with others. Record these thoughts and reflections.

♥ Don't carry the burden of your quest for everlasting love inside of you. Share what you are trying to accomplish with trusted friends or advisors. Since overcoming the regrets of past love relationships is key to your success in the future, having the courage to include past friends and lovers in your 30 Day Plan of Action is not only admirable but can be immensely beneficial.

♥ Incorporating more fun activities into your schedule for Week Two will help you focus and evaluate your progress towards greater self-confidence. It will also make you decisively face your fears and regrets about past relationships within a social environment.

♥ As you approach the halfway mark in our 30 Day Plan of Action, make sure you are ready and grounded enough to take the next steps towards your everlasting love. Continue on the positive path of self-assurance and the awareness you have initiated. Soul-searching should be a daily exercise. Social interaction should become more comfortable as you observe others (and yourself) in a less judgmental, more analytical way.

STEP FOUR
Raising Your Self Esteem

"Love is the great miracle cure. Loving ourselves works miracles in our lives."

Louise Hay

"To love oneself is the beginning of a lifelong romance."

Oscar Wilde

What positive attitude is:

Positive attitude is the latent power you have within you to bring about what you want. It is your own personal "happy face" designed just for you. A positive attitude is your ally; it is on your side no matter what. That's the reason you decide to look for it and adopt it. Think of that happy face as an animated character that jumps into your arms and looks admiringly up at you, longing to bring you a brighter outlook. That happy face wants to make you happy, not just lift you up.

What positive attitude is not:

Positive attitude is not hoping-against-hope. But being positive does mean that you can take your "divine discontentment", and use it as a springboard to a better lifestyle that does bring you contentment. Hoping and wishing won't get you there, though. But being certain within yourself that you can be a loving and happy person is taking a positive action. Changing your attitude is action; hoping is merely daydreaming. You "hope" he or she will call; you "hope" he or she will ask you out. What can you do to move the process along? Well, you can put him or her on the back burner and go out with someone else; let your answer machine do the waiting for you. That is positive attitude, taking action and not merely hoping. Looking to see the built-in solution in any problem constitutes a positive action, one that causes you to think and act creatively. And creative thinking will yield positive results, and that will give you confidence. "Hoping" will only bring you a passive feeling of helplessness unless you take affirmative action in your mind.

Real-Life Revelation:

What you did or did not do in past involvements cannot be changed. What can be changed is the attitude you carry with you in your search for everlasting love. You can choose to view the past differently, for starters. Look back and mentally change the outcome of an involvement that went wrong. That's what Mark did. "I carried around a lot of hurt and guilt over my failed marriage," Mark said. "But I got tired of thinking myself a failure, just because I was young and ignorant when I married. So I reran the marriage in my mind. I imagined how I would have done things differently had I, and my wife, been more mature. Once I did this, I felt okay and I thought, 'Gee, I can have a good relationship; it's not so terrifying'."

Positive attitude is about living for today and creating a new "head set" for a more fulfilling future. One of my favorite affirmations is so simple because it doesn't antagonize the mind.   Write down what you want to occur in your life, using this thought: "It's possible that *blank* can happen." Fill in the *blank* and see how easy it is. "It's possible that *everlasting love* can happen to me." "It's possible that *success and happiness* can happen to me."   This affirmation is exciting to me because it focuses on possibilities, not limitations. And it is wide open; you can fill in that blank with as many things as you desire your mind to accept. No matter what restrictions you imposed or encountered in the past, this affirmation can help you move past them and design a new relationship-life.

Creating a positive attitude in yourself is just one side of the coin. The other side is creating a positive attitude in the people you encounter. No, you cannot change other people. But you can change the way you view them, and they will most likely respond to your positive notions. Visualize the good in other people, no matter how offensive they may appear to you. No, you don't have to put up with offensive behavior; that's not what we are talking about here. You are using your visualization power for them, just as you use it for yourself. Picture, imagine, absorb yourself in how you want that person to be in your presence. Imagine a favorable outcome when talking with that person. Extract that person's positive qualities and enhance them in your mind. If nothing else, you will have opened a door for dialogue. And who knows, that "negative" person may just become very positive by being around you.

How to maintain a positive attitude:

Practice not only makes perfect, it perfects what it makes. Try a little experiment, just to keep you on the positive track. For five minutes each day, close the mental doors on every negative thought that comes into your mind and replace them with positive thoughts. After a month, you will have conditioned yourself to automatically shut out thoughts that tear you down. For instance, if you meet someone you would like to know better and your mind says, "You'll never have a chance," stop the thought right there. Replace it with "I have the confidence to socialize with that person, and what do I have to lose?" The answer is: Nothing. What do you have to gain? Everything.

Another exercise in positive attitude is to look in the mirror and tell yourself what you want to hear. This is especially powerful if you live alone and don't get enough compliments from other people. Give those compliments to yourself. That person in the mirror is the most important person you will ever know; his or her opinion is really all that matters in the long run.

EXERCISES
STEP 4

Exercise #1: **Reflections.** Use the space below to record your thoughts as you begin Week Two.

_____

_____

_____

_____

Exercise #2: **Qualities.** List the best qualities you have to bring to a relationship.

_____

_____

_____

Exercise #3: **Be nice to yourself.** Pamper yourself every day. Take a bubble bath, have some ice cream (go ahead, splurge!), go for a long walk, take a nap. Everyday during this week, do sweet little things for yourself.

Exercise #4: **Weekly treat.** Once this week, do something really special, something you've always wanted to do or something you haven't done in a long time to prove to yourself that you are valuable. (Get a massage, go to the theater, buy that dress or sport coat you've told yourself you can't afford.)

Exercise #5: **Success.** What do you feel is the biggest success you have achieved in life?

_____

_____

_____

_____

_____

_____

_____

_____

Exercise #6: **Failure.** What do you feel is the biggest failure or drawback you have ever experienced?

_____

_____

_____

_____

Exercise #7: **What is holding you back?** Write down your fears that have prevented you from reaching your goals.

_____

_____

_____

_____

Exercise #8: **Challenges.** Make a list of challenges you have recently confronted, and describe how you dealt with them.

_____

_____

_____

_____

Use the following space for additional notes.

Ava's
Pearls
of Wisdom

"Wealth is inherited, but respect and wisdom are always earned."

STEP 5
Appreciating Qualities You Bring To A Relationship

*"To love someone deeply
gives you strength...
Being loved by someone deeply
gives you courage."*

Lao Tzu

Step 5: Perceive all the positive elements of your personality and lifestyle.

Recognizing the qualities you bring to a relationship is imperative, and it's also a good idea to work on qualities that you would like to improve.

Step 5 is about taking an inventory of both the gifts you bring to a potential partnership and the areas in which you need to improve. For many people, this is the hardest step of all. If there is one defining reason why people don't get what they want in their lives, it's because they don't really think they deserve it.

Well, you do deserve to have the life of your dreams, but you might have to take a deep, deep look in the mirror and see a brand new you looking back. You have the power and potential to create a truly fulfilling life which includes having the partner of your dreams. See the power, for it is there.

If you had to sell your car today, you'd be able to point out all of its good points. You know it's not perfect but you'd play up the new paint job, the fuel efficient engine, the low mileage, and so on. If you can sell a piece of metal, you can sell yourself.

Maybe there are things that need improvement, but so what? You have what it takes to admit these things and to change them!

"A loving person lives in a loving world. A hostile person lives in a hostile world. Everyone you meet is your mirror."

Ken Keyes, Jr.

Exercise #1: **Benefits.** Write down the benefits you derive from being in a relationship (e.g. companionship, security, stability, etc.):

_____

_____

_____

_____

Exercise #2: **Agent.** Pretend you're an agent whose job it is to sell you to a prospective date (or mate). Be sure to include your positive qualities and summarize the attributes you can bring to a relationship. For example, if I were an agent selling Dr. Ava Cadell, I might say: "She is compassionate, quite articulate, has a wonderful sense of humor, is very creative, spiritual, kind, sensitive, sophisticated and loves helping people. You've got to meet her!" (Whatever you do, don't use words like nice. Really sell your client — you.)

_____

_____

_____

_____

_____

Exercise #3: **Improvements.** Make a list of personal improvements and changes you are willing to make in order to attract your "everlasting love." These improvements can be physical, intellectual, emotional or spiritual. Examples: Get in shape, take a course in communication, buy new clothes, have a more positive attitude, etc.

_____

_____

_____

_____

Exercise #4: **Won't change.** Make a list of those inner qualities and attitudes that you are not willing to change or compromise for "everlasting love." Example: I am not willing to change my independence, my love for travel, my love for pets, etc.

_____

_____

_____

Exercise #5: **Dealing with people.** Name five things you feel you are good at accomplishing in dealing with people. Example: Patient, good negotiator, good listener, polite, etc.

_____

_____

_____

_____

Exercise #6: **How do you exercise your mind?** (by reading, writing, watching TV, meditation, etc.)

_____

_____

_____

Exercise #7: **How do you exercise your body?** (by stretching, lifting weights, sports, aeorobics, etc.)

_____

_____

_____

_____

Exercise #8: **Write yourself a love letter.** Be sure to include all the qualities that make you special.

_____
_____
_____
_____
_____
_____
_____
_____
_____
_____
_____
_____
_____

Use the following space for additional notes.

Ava's
Pearls
of Wisdom

"Kind words and good deeds are eternal. You never know where their influence will take you."

STEP 6
Determining The Qualities You Are Looking For

"It is only with the heart
that one can see rightly;
what is essential
is invisible to the eye."

Antoine de Saint-Exupery

Step 6: Compile and prioritize those qualities you are seeking in a partner.

If you don't know who you're looking for, you won't recognize them when you meet them!
Step 6 is all about declaring what you want. I know you've heard the saying, "You can't get what you want unless you ask for it."

You're in the driver's seat. Instead of hoping that your twin souls find you in the midst of the teeming masses, instead of praying that God takes care of all this, instead of sitting shoulder-to-shoulder with other love victims, drinking Long Island iced teas and complaining about the lack of good men/women "out there," pretend you are in charge.

Imagine you are looking to buy a car. There are hundreds of different cars on the market, because not everyone wants the same thing. Do you want a compact, a station wagon or a sports car? Stick shift or automatic? Are you looking for fast and sleek or economical and safe? Maybe something in between? You know what you'd like in a car, now think about what you'd like in a partner.

What kind of partner are you looking for? There are as many kinds of relationships as there are cars. This is not the time to settle for second best. What qualities do you want in a partner?

You should have a better idea by now of what you bring to a relationship.

"Many people will walk in and out of your life, But only true friends will leave footprints in your heart."
Eleanor Roosevelt

Exercise #1: **Relationship.** Write down what kind of relationship you are looking for, e.g. friendship, long-term lover, marriage, family, etc.:

_____

Exercise #2: **Personal ad.** Pretend you're writing a personal ad to find your ideal mate. Include all the qualities as well as the attributes you are looking for. Use as many words as you need. Be specific. For example: "Intelligent, well-educated, has a great sense of humor, is interested in culture, likes to learn new things, likes socializing, is well-built, eats healthy, exercises regularly, is financially responsible, loves to read, believes in God, enjoys meditation, loves music, loves pets, etc."

_____

_____

_____

_____

Exercise #3: **Admiration list: Opposite sex.** Name three people of the opposite sex you most admire. These can be famous people, friends or relatives:

_____

_____

Exercise #4: **Admiration list: Same sex.** Name three people of the same sex you admire. Admirable traits in your own sex might be items that need to be improved or added to your own persona.

_____

_____

_____

_____

Exercise #5: **Attributes.** List the personal attributes and/or accomplishments of the above individuals, and detail those traits which make them so admirable to you (e.g. Jane Fonda is ambitious, sexy, independent, strong-willed, etc.). The attributes you have listed as the ones you find attractive can become the qualities you seek in your everlasting love.

_____

_____

_____

_____

Use space below for additional notes.

Ava's Pearls of Wisdom

"Joy is contagious. People never tire of being in the company of a happy person."

Worksheet Week Two ~ Monday:

Begin the day with self-image reinforcement in front of my mirror. Focus on the positive aspects of my body. What do I see? Give myself as many compliments as I can every day.

_____

_____

What did I do to pamper or reward myself today?

_____

_____

What are the positive things I did for other people today?

_____

_____

What new qualities did I use today that I observed from watching others?

_____

_____

Where did I spend my social time? With whom and why?

_____

_____

_____

Did I see any qualities in anyone that I would want in a partner? If so, what qualities did I see that I liked?

_____

_____

What self-improvements did I accomplish today?

_____

_____

_____

Describe the events of the day. Note if I have started to incorporate some of the attributes I observed in others.

_____

_____

_____

_____

Use the space below for additional notes.

*Ava's
Pearls
of Wisdom*

Compliments are
the bedrock of
romance so give
them freely.

Worksheet Week Two ~ Tuesday:

Begin the day with self-image reinforcement in front of my mirror. Focus on the positive aspects of my body. What do I see? Give myself as many compliments as I can every day.

_____

_____

What did I do to pamper or reward myself today?

_____

What are the positive things I did for other people today?

_____

_____

What new qualities did I use today that I observed from watching others?

_____

_____

Where did I spend my social time? With whom and why?

_____

_____

_____

_____

What self-improvements did I accomplish today?

_____

_____

_____

_____

Describe the events of the day. Note if I have started to incorporate some of the attributes I observed in others. What made me feel good today?

_____

_____

_____

_____

What could I have done today to be more productive?

_____

_____

_____

Use the space below for additional notes.

Ava's
Pearls
of Wisdom

The important
thing is not what
others think of
you, but what
you think of you.

Worksheet Week Two ~ Wednesday:

Begin the day with self-image reinforcement in front of my mirror. Focus on the positive aspects of my body. What do I see? Give myself as many compliments as I can every day.

_____

_____

What did I do to pamper or reward myself today?

_____

What are the positive things I did for other people today?

_____

_____

What new qualities did I use today that I observed from watching others?

_____

Where did I spend my social time? With whom and why?

_____

_____

What self-improvements did I accomplish today?

_____

_____

Describe the events of the day. Note if I have started to incorporate some of the attributes I observed in others.

_____

_____

_____

What would I change about today's events if I could?

_____

_____

_____

Use the space below for additional notes.

*Ava's
Pearls
of Wisdom*

It's never too late
to heal an injured
relationship.

Worksheet Week Two ~ Thursday:

Begin the day with self-image reinforcement in front of my mirror. Focus on the positive aspects of my body. What do I see? Give myself as many compliments as I can every day.

_____

_____

What did I do to pamper or reward myself today?

_____

_____

It would be a relief for me if I could only:

_____

_____

What new qualities did I use today that I observed from watching others?

_____

_____

Where did I spend my social time? With whom and why?

_____

_____

_____

_____

I was irritated today when:

_____

_____

Describe the events of the day. Note if I have started to incorporate some of the attributes I observed in others.

_____

_____

What was the most important thing that happened to me today and why?

_____

_____

_____

Use the space below for additional notes.

*Ava's
Pearls
of Wisdom*

You shouldn't
expect life's
very best,
if you're not giving
it your
very best.

Worksheet Week Two ~ Friday:

Begin the day with self-image reinforcement in front of my mirror. Focus on the positive aspects of my body. What do I see? Give myself as many compliments as I can every day.

_____

_____

What did I do to pamper or reward myself today?

_____

_____

What are the positive things I did for other people today?

_____

_____

What positive things did someone do for me today?

_____

_____

My only regret today was:

_____

_____

The funniest thing that happened to me today was:

_____

_____

The best words to describe today's events are:

_____

_____

_____

My biggest obstacle today was:

_____

_____

Use the space below for additional notes.

Ava's Pearls of Wisdom

It's not possible to achieve everything in life without the help & support of others.

Worksheet Week Two ~ Saturday:

Begin the day with self-image reinforcement in front of my mirror. Focus on the positive aspects of my body. What do I see? Continue to give myself as many compliments as I can every day.

_____

_____

What did I do to pamper or reward myself today?

_____

_____

I was most comfortable today when:

_____

_____

I felt powerful today when:

_____

_____

The most interesting person I met today was:

_____

_____

Today I wish I had more:

_____

_____

Today I wish I had less:

_____

_____

_____

What did my body language portray today?

_____

_____

_____

Use the space below for additional notes.

Ava's
Pearls of
Wisdom

Learn to love
yourself and
others will love you
too.

Worksheet Week Two ~ Sunday:

Begin the day with self-image reinforcement in front of my mirror. Focus on the positive aspects of my body. What do I see? Give myself as many compliments as I can every day.

_____

_____

_____

What did I do to pamper or reward myself today?

_____

_____

The person I would have liked to spend more time with today was:

_____

_____

If there was one question I would have asked someone today it would have been:

_____

_____

My greatest fear today was:

_____

_____

_____

What self-improvements did I accomplish today?

_____

_____

Describe the events of the day. Note if I have started to incorporate some of the attributes I observed in others.

_____

_____

_____

_____

What was my biggest accomplishment this week?

_____

_____

_____

Use the space below for additional notes.

Ava's
Pearls
of Wisdom

The best
tranquilizer
is a clear conscience.

At the End of Week Two:

Preview Steps 7, 8 and 9 and review Steps 1-6 before you begin Week Three. The first week of the 12 Steps to Everlasting Love was dedicated to healing. Week Two was focused on self-value. Week Three is all about finding your everlasting love. For most of us, these are the bravest steps. Once we have a clear idea of what we want in a mate, we need to know where to find him or her, the methods of approach and how to be prepared for the dating process. Fasten your seat belt! If you allow it to be, this next part of 12 Steps to Everlasting Love can be a whole lot of fun!

WEEK THREE
Finding Everlasting Love

Pessimism is an important predictor of problems, just as optimism is an important predictor of success."
Gavin de Becker

Steps 7 through 9 are action steps to finding everlasting love.

Now that you know who you are looking for, where are you going to find that person? You don't go looking for a golfer at a swimming pool.

I had a client who said to me, "I don't know why all the men I date are alcoholics." Can you guess where she met all her dates? In a bar, of course.

Step 7 is about developing a strategy, taking the initiative and going for broke. Great things seldom just fall into our laps. We help them happen. In any arena, you must first set a goal (what kind of life partner do you want?), before you can realize your dreams. Next, you develop a strategy (where would this partner be found and how can you get the response you want?), and then you kick into action.

Remember that the best places to go are where you will be outnumbered by the opposite sex. For example, to meet women take a dance or yoga class or attend a relationship seminar. To meet men, go to sporting events, a hardware store or attend a business seminar. To meet a lawyer, try a courthouse. To meet a doctor, have lunch in the hospital cafeteria.

Happy hunting!

Sex is one of the greatest gifts to the human race. Sharing yourself with someone worthy of your affection and trust is the most precious thing one can give to another."
Dr. Ava Cadell

Instructions

Week Three ~ FINDING EVERLASTING LOVE

Step 7: Finding Your Everlasting Love
Step 8: Approaching & Maintaining Communication
Step 9: Evaluating Your Dating Expectations

Week Three Instructions:

Steps 7-9

This is a critical week. It is a symbolic week, representative of your future. Your life mate, your everlasting love, is out there. You must open yourself to the opportunities of meeting new people and creating a persona that will ensure the success of your quest.

Daily reinforcement of the 12 Steps Philosophy is the key element to achieving your goal of everlasting love. Steps 1-6 are still as important as they were in the earlier two weeks.

~NEW~ projects as you begin Week Three:

❤ Your commitment to social time should be stronger as you enter your third week. Turn that one day or night you have devoted to fun into a full 24 hour-day and night, devoid of work or home responsibilities.

❤ Incorporate one situation that, in the past, proved to be difficult. See that you are able to handle the same situation with renewed perspective and acceptance.

❤ Take the plunge and ask out that person you have been secretly admiring. If accepted, incorporate as many of the personal traits and mannerisms you have been admiring in others over the past few weeks into your own behavior.

❤ If your date proposal is rejected, realize that you can survive it. Your target rejected the situation, not you! It is far better not to waste time on someone who is unavailable or uninterested. Move on to the next prospect!

By the end of this third week you should be able to better understand both yourself and others in a clearer and more positive light. With the wisdom and added insight gleaned from adherence to the 30-Day Plan-of-Action, you are now ready for the final tasks of the program, the last roundup. Take time to recognize that the principles utilized herein are ones that will (and must) stay with you forever.

♥ Your self-image enhancement and positive affirmations should, by now, be part of your daily routine. Continue to write down three affirmations each morning and repeat them to yourself throughout the day.

♥ Write down two more fun things that you would like to do or two new places you would like to visit, and add them to your list from the previous two weeks. At this point it's expected that you will include at least two or more of these activities in your schedule for Week Three.

♥ Increase your level of confidence by making a conscious effort to greet others with a sincere smile and kind words: strangers, co-workers, associates and friends. Share your good thoughts with at least three people every day.

♥ Continue your observations of both sexes. Review the list of traits and features you admire in others. Prioritize entries in the order in which they seem most important. Remember to keep two lists. One list is made up of attributes you seek in your everlasting love. The second list is comprised of traits that you have admired in others and have tried to incorporate into your own behavior.

♥ Make sure you begin to allocate more daily time for that non-work/non-home social interaction. It's fine to   continue to share this time with a close friend for support, but now you may want to take this opportunity to offer that social invitation to someone new. If your offer is rebuffed, don't loose your confidence. Dating is a numbers game. The more often you make an approach, the more practice you will have, and practice makes perfect.

♥ Note the results of your efforts to meet others. What good thoughts were shared? Did you use any of the flirting techniques? Which did you find effective?

♥ Describe the events of the day. Make observations of your behavior, as well as that of others, in your social situations.

Places To Meet Someone?

Airplanes	Hardware Stores	Religious Services
At Work	Health Clubs	Restaurants
Auction Houses	Home Building Centers	Reunions
Bars	Jogging	Seminars
Beaches	Jury Duty	Shopping Malls
Bike Riding	Libraries	Singles Events
Bookstores	Matchmakers	Sports Events
Bridge Clubs	Men's Departments	Supermarkets
Cafes	Movies	Theater Groups
Car Wash	Museums	Through Friends
Classes	Outdoor Festivals	Through Relatives
Computer Networks	Parks	Trade Shows
Dance Clubs	Parties	Twelve Steps Meetings
Day Trips	Personal Ads	Vacations
Fashion Shows	Pot Lucks	Volunteer Work
Flea Markets	Public Lectures	Walking
Galleries	Readings	Weddings

How To Flirt

1. Eye Contact
   Glance, don't stare
   Raise your eyebrows
   Wink if you're bold

2. Smile
   A warm sincere smile is like an open door of approval

3. Body Language
   The Hair Flip   Head Toss
   Leg Swinging   The Lean
   Utensil Playfulness   The Lip Lick
   Hand Signals   The Toast (your glass)

4. Flirting Props
   Carry a book with an eye-catching title
   Wear a hat that suits your style
   Pin a button on your clothes that has a message to attract attention
   Take your pet for a walk, no matter what it is
   Carry a camera and ask if you can take someone's picture for your office
   Apply an outrageous bumper sticker to your car
   Wear clothes with unusual logos
   Drive a unique car or bike

STEP 7
Finding Your Everlasting Love

"Miracles occur naturally as expressions of love.
The real miracle is the love that inspires them.
In this sense everything that comes from love is a miracle."

Marianne Williamson

EXERCISES
STEP 7

Exercise #1: **Priorities.** From the personal ad and admiration exercises in Step 6, prioritize the qualities and attributes that you are looking for.

_____

_____

_____

Exercise #2: **Where are they?** Where are you going to meet more people? List the places you're going to go this week:

_____

_____

Exercise #3: **New people.** Set a goal regarding how many people you're going to meet by this time (a) Next week (b) Next month

_____

_____

_____

Exercise #4: **Support.** What kind of support system will ensure your success? (a) Buddy system (b) Group meetings (c) Other

_____

_____

Describe and elaborate:

_____

_____

_____

Exercise #5: **Initiative.** List how you're going to initiate meetings. For example: Take out personal ads, tell friends and family, join social groups, etc.

_____

_____

Exercise #6: **Attraction.** Smile at someone you are attracted to. Extend a greeting to a stranger. Compliment at least 3 people.

_____

_____

_____

Exercise #7: **My perfect date.** Write a description of your perfect first date from start to finish in as much detail as possible.

_____

_____

_____

_____

_____

_____

_____

_____

_____

_____

_____

_____

_____

_____

_____

STEP 8
Approaching And Maintaining Communication

"Lack of communication is like having a car without fuel.
It will still be a car but it will not be able to go anywhere."

Dr. Ava Cadell

The Art of Communication

"A lasting relationship must have friendship, passion, respect, trust, and communication."

Dr. Ava Cadell

What communication is:

Communication is the real, honest-to-goodness relating that leads to genuine intimacy and a healthy bond between two people. And, good communication leads to good sex that will only get better as a couple gets to know each other more deeply. If you're in a relationship that you don't want to be in, there's probably little communication. But if you're in a relationship that works, my sense is that you have good communication. In my years as a sex educator and counselor, I have noticed that there are many roadblocks and problems preventing people from having a consistently successful love life. One of the most common is the lack of communication or improper communication.

Isn't it great that communication isn't confined to just words, though? That makes it so much more fun to explore this subject, especially when you want to have a new adventure with your partner, erotic or otherwise. Communication is reflected in our voice tone, body movements and our speech patterns. Communication is even conveyed by what we don't say, sometimes. Communication can be subtle, too; you don't always have to be hit over the head with an anvil to get the point. A partner's raised eyebrow may be sufficient to indicate a whole range of meanings, such as surprise, contempt, glee, superiority or annoyance.

Relationships that grow, evolve and are the most emotionally and sexually fulfilling all have this secret ingredient of communication binding them together. Why is communication like a secret ingredient? Because it involves opening up all our five senses, and then some. To utilize this secret ingredient, we must be open to what information our senses are conveying, and then translate that input into words. Openness is the key word! Remember the magic words Ali Baba used in the Arabian Nights to open the door of the robbers' den, so he could get to the treasures inside? "Open sesame." That fairy tale term has become a modern buzz word for "gaining admission"; it is a secret password. Ali Baba knew the secret of communication: Be willing to use the password, and be willing to "open". Ali Baba didn't know all that he would find behind that door. He didn't even know for sure if the password would work. But he was open.

How to change your perception of communication:

What we really want to know is, "Am I getting across the way I intend"? We all grew up in families that communicated in certain ways, whether effectively or not. We are comfortable with the communication patterns we learned at home. We often don't think about growing beyond that point, yet it may be vital in a relationship. In your career life, you have to keep up with modern technology to stay afloat, much less to get ahead. Our relationships should be just as important. Don't be afraid to learn how the other person communicates. How did your partner's family relate to each other, and can you glean something from their communication patterns that you can add to your own "communications repertoire"?

Positive Communication

This "dating game" stage of a relationship, the first few months, should keep its focus on positive communication. Find out about each other. Use questions to draw each other out. Focus on your commonalities and how they can enhance your relationship. Talking is very important during this stage, but listening is equally as vital. Rewarding each other with positive feedback, compliments and reassurances can set the stage for closer contact. Get to know what one another likes first and then savor the verbal foreplay. Do talk about your hobbies, places you like to go, positive aspects of your family and friends, your work, goals and aspirations. Don't talk about old relationships, problems, money or sex on a first date.

Intimate Communication

Remember, communication is the number one ingredient for a consistently successful love life. The second rule of thumb is "say what you feel". Saying what you feel is giving audible language to the flow of feelings, discovering and articulating those emotions that are the constant undercurrent of our lives. Revealing these emotions is a way for you to continue to endear yourself to your partner. We often think that intimacy is created merely by chemistry or by what we do, plan or pursue together. But, it is actually getting to know another person through his or her emotions that makes us feel truly connected. So if you want to move from dating to intimacy, communicate your intentions. For example, would you ask your date how they like their coffee? Of course you would. So then, why wouldn't you ask your partner how they like to be touched? The fact is that most people either think that their partner will automatically like what they like sexually, or they think their partner should be able to read their mind. Find out about your dates "romantic list." Do they relish in eating bon bons by the fireplace, snuggling up with popcorn and a movie, caviar and toast points or does getting their head massaged make them feel loving? It's up to you to discover their secret romantic list.

Here is the opportunity to explore the passionate power of words. Before becoming intimate, before having sex with your partner for the first time, find out what each of you likes in bed. This is a level where both of you will feel sensitive. If you are about to take the plunge, talk about your needs more openly. Certainly if you were preparing a steak for your partner, you would ask your partner how he or she likes it cooked. After all, you wouldn't want to ruin a good piece of meat. So why risk the demise of a perfectly good relationship?

It can be difficult to talk about sex because we aren't given courses in school on how to do it. And most likely, our parents didn't give us much help in this area, either. We plunge into relationships expecting our partners to know our needs by osmosis, and that's rather presumptuous, isn't it? How can we expect someone else to know where to touch us if we don't find a positive way to tell them? In love-making, we are totally on our own; maybe that's why it can feel so awkward to express what we want and find out about our partner's desires and needs. But we may fear rejection or be afraid we can't measure up.

No ironclad rules exist to fall back upon; we just have to "wing it" and "risk it". And maybe that's a good thing — if it opens us up to talk more freely. If you were lost in a foreign city, you would certainly seek out someone you could talk to and ask about directions. You would be just as vulnerable in that situation, too. Asking for directions in love-making is just part of getting where you want to go.

We aren't just dealing with erotic needs at this level, but intimate, nurturing needs. If it feels scary to ask for erotic nurturing, first tell one another how much you respect him or her and how you want to please each other. Ask each other about turn-ons in the way of lovemaking. Go slowly; the more time you take, the more excitement you build up and the more barriers you break down. Tantalize your partner with the possibility you can fulfill each other's wildest dreams and fantasies. Verbal foreplay is extremely important at this stage. You might say things like "You look so inviting lying there like that, it makes me want to kiss you from head to toe." Tell each other the little things that feel good or entice, such as, "I love your smile and that's such a turn-on to me," or "It feels so sexy when you lightly finger-massage my back."

Give each other positive feedback during and after love-making. Feel free to ask that your needs be met; express what you need by saying things like, "I need to be held close after making love," or "I just can't get enough oral sex from you. I love the feeling of surrender when you take me in your mouth". And if your partner is reluctant to open up, then ask, ask, ask in a gentle and loving way. Ask what his/her deepest desires are, and how you can meet them. And if that first love-making session isn't everything you want, tell each other in a positive way what turns you on and what doesn't. Instead of saying,

"You chewed on my ears as if they were made out of beef jerky", you could say, "I really enjoyed it when you kissed and licked my ears gently".

How to Say "No"

Let's also look at a healthy way to say "no" without hurting your lover's feelings. Even the best relationships have bad days, so here are a couple of tips on how to de-escalate conflict and make it easier to attain resolution. I want to give you a simple two-step process in which you acknowledge what your partner wants, then you negotiate and compromise by using positive reinforcement.

Step 1: Instead of blaming your partner with sentences that begin with "you", try saying "I feel", and let your partner see your vulnerability and hurt. Here's a common example: "You always go to sleep after we make love, and I'm frustrated." A better way to express this would be: "I love making love to you; you make me feel so good. Maybe next time we make love, we can spend some time cuddling because it means so much to me when you hold me in your arms before you fall asleep."

Step 2: Listen to your partner when he/she is expressing feelings, then repeat what your partner said using your own words. Your partner will either agree with your translation or will correct you. Once it's clear, you can state your own point of view and repeat the process. Let's pretend your partner is saying this: "I'm really feeling insecure lately, because you don't spend as much time kissing me as you once did. I know we have sex all the time but I really miss the intimacy of kissing." Now, repeat in your own words what you think your partner is saying here. Perhaps your partner wants more affection or reassurance. By telling your partner what you think he/she means, you open a line of communication and that can bring you closer together. Also, remember these three pointers when dealing with you partner: 1) Presume your mate is innocent until proven guilty. 2) Be curious rather than furious. 3) Try to understand your partner's actions from his/her point of view.

Once two people have connected in an intimate way, the relationship changes course. We all feel more vulnerable after sex has entered into the picture. The union either grows stronger at this point, or interest in each other wanes. If you can talk and be more open with each other, the sexual intimacy goes to a deeper level and gets better and better. But if you emotionally distance each other, the relationship can end.

Physical, Mental and Spiritual Communication

This is the deepest form of communication. At this level of your relationship, you are becoming attuned to each other's physical needs, you have that blissful mind-to-mind connection and you feel that soul-mate resonance. But couples often revert to Level One at this point, because they've made the conquest or they're married and don't feel a need to keep trying. It is of extreme value at this level to keep investing in the relationship. It is imperative to set aside one hour of communication time each day, to keep current on each other's needs and to know each other more deeply. Don't take the relationship for granted just because you have secured each other. Continue to do spontaneous little things for the one you love, and find out if he or she likes new adventures, new interests. One couple I know was together for five years before they discovered they both liked roller-skating. This added a new zest to their relationship.

You never know what surprises that one hour per day can bring you. And it can really secure everlasting love between the two of you, more so than presuming everything is okay. Your connection with each other will keep growing on all levels.

Moving beyond communication

The way to move beyond communication is through more communication. Then we no longer fear talking to each other. It becomes as natural as breathing. If we have feared rejection, intimacy, inadequacy, and being able to talk about and deal with these very common problems, then more and better communication can't hurt. It can only improve any situation. Even if your partner tells you a little more than you wanted to know, that provides you with yet another topic for discussion. Then you can clear the air and move on.

"Communicate your needs, wants and desires because your partner cannot read your mind."

Dr. Ava Cadell

Step 8: Conversation, Like a Relationship, Involves Both Listening and Talking.

How many times have you seen someone you wanted to meet but couldn't think of anything to say? Then they vanished and you wanted to kick yourself! First impressions are important, but it's not the end of the world if you don't have a great opening line to impress someone. You do, however, have to say something. Why do you think people talk about the weather so much?

The easiest and most effective conversation starter is to give a compliment. Then follow it with a question to maintain the conversation. And you can always talk about the environment you're both in. Remember, the more interested you are in people, the more interesting you are to them. Be a good listener and find common ground.

Everyone has something conversational to tell you. Your mission is to find out what it is. It could be anything — where they are from, why they chose that tie, or what they had for breakfast. Any open-ended question will do. Pretend you're a journalist interviewing them. Ideally, you both should be asking each other and answering one another's questions. In this way, the conversation never gets to that awkward "now what?" stage.

Secrets Of Conversation

Now that you have some guidance on how to get a conversation started, it's important to recognize that not only words but also voice-quality is an important ingredient in heightening the impact and effectiveness of your conversation. It also helps to be aware that people are particular in the way they like to communicate, primarily as represented by (1) "visual" or image-stimulation, (2) "kinesthetic" or feeling-stimulation and, (3) "auditory" or sound-stimulation.

Visual people want to know how they look. They want to see images and they like to look at the person talking to them. They also enjoy someone who speaks with passion and has lots of expression in their voice. Visual people want to be admired for how good they look. They want to be seen as sexy, beautiful or handsome. Tell them, "You look great" or "Your hair looks shiny and beautiful."

Kinesthetic people are feeling oriented. They like to be held, touched, stroked and to hear what you are feeling and sensing. They relish the emotional feelings of words and favor slow, sensuous dialogue. Tell a kinesthetic person, "I feel good being with you" or "Your skin feels like silk."

Auditory people are good listeners and like the sound of words. They enjoy great detail and will often analyze what you have said. The tone of your voice is important and the inflections used in a sentence can often make the difference between ordinary or extraordinary communication. Give an auditory person a lot of information about "why, what and how." "I love being around you because you make me feel so good."

Good communication involves all three of these modalities, but your best chance of "making a good first impression" depends on your ability to recognize the effect your words are having on your "intended." Ask that new person some basic questions, and then pay particular attention to the responses.

When you open a conversation with someone new, the words you choose to open that first conversation can be the most important words you will ever speak, especially as part of your quest for "finding everlasting love." And remember that the words and actions that are necessary to communicate your feelings and intentions in a continuing dialogue with that special person will depend on your perceptions and reactions to the words and actions of your partner.

"To receive everything, one must open one's hands and give."
Taisen Deshimaru

Conversation Starters

1. The Friendly Approach
Can be used on anyone.

- I'm really kind of shy, but I saw you and knew I had to get over myself and meet you.
- Excuse me, can you tell me the best way to meet someone like you?
- I just wanted to come over and introduce myself, because I have the feeling that I'll see you again.
- You look like someone I should know.
- Hi, can we pretend that I used some line that worked really well and move on to the next stage?
- You look like the kind of person I would really like to get to know better.
- Could I borrow part of your newspaper that you're not reading.
- I love your tie/jacket/dress. Where did you get it?

2. The Humorous Approach
There's no better response than making someone laugh.

- I'm tired of people wanting me for my brain and not my body. Can you help me?
- Do you have a boyfriend/girlfriend with a Mustang? (name your car) Well, you do now.
- Hi, my name is Chance. Do I have one?
- Do you believe in love at first sight, or do I have to walk by you again?
- I've lost my phone number, can I borrow yours?
- Hi, I'm Mr. Right. Someone said you were looking for me.
- My dog would like to meet your dog, but she's very shy.

3. The Seductive Approach
Should stir, not shock!

- ❤ You smell really good. What scent are you wearing?
- ❤ Weren't you in the Sports Illustrated swimsuit issue?
- ❤ Didn't I see you on the cover of GQ magazine?
- ❤ I hope you don't mind, but I just had to let you know that you are the sexiest person here.
- ❤ Do you mind if I sit down? When I saw you I went weak in the knees.
- ❤ If good looks were against the law, you'd be arrested, booked and jailed for life.
- ❤ Can I buy you breakfast in the morning?
- ❤ I was looking in the dictionary, and there isn't a word that fully describes your beauty/sex appeal.

4. The Offbeat Approach
Can command lots of attention.

- ❤ I'm doing a poll on where single people like to go. Can you help me?
- ❤ I'm collecting photos of the best dressed people for a project. Could I take your picture, please?
- ❤ I'm writing an article on how single people like to flirt. Can you help me?
- ❤ I just had new shocks put on my car. Care to help me test them?
- ❤ I finally met a girl I can take home to mom. So what are you doing Sunday?
- ❤ Can I have your autograph? I'm your biggest fan. Don't forget your phone number.

Opening Lines Should Include: A compliment, a question, a statement about your environment, and an introduction

EXERCISES
STEP 8

Exercise #1: **Lifestyle.** Write down questions you can ask to find out if someone will fit into your lifestyle. Examples: What do you like to do for fun? What are your favorite foods?

_____

_____

_____

_____

Exercise #2: **Opening lines.** Write down three opening lines to begin a conversation with someone:
(a) A friendly line

_____

_____

(b) A humorous line

_____

_____

(c) A seductive line

_____

_____

Exercise #3: **More opening lines.** Write down three more opening lines focusing on:
(a) A compliment

_____

_____

(b) A question

_____

_____

(c) A statement about the environment you're both in

_____

_____

_____

_____

Exercise #4: **Flirting.** How do you like people to flirt with you?

(a) Eye Contact   (b) Body language   (c) Conversation   (d) Other

Describe and elaborate.
_____
_____
_____

Exercise #5: **Flirting.** Begin to flirt with people you find attractive. Take along flirting props and use the techniques previously discussed. What flirting props do you have?
_____
_____
_____
_____

Exercise #6: **Making a date.** Continue the conversation by asking more open ended questions, and end the conversation by either making a date or getting a phone number. Write down some open-ended questions.
_____
_____
_____

Exercise #7: **Flirting skills.** What are you going to do to improve your flirting skills?
_____
_____
_____
_____
_____
_____
_____

Four Dating Rules

No, the love of your life is most likely not going to come to your front door and present a calling card saying, "I am your everlasting love". I do know of one woman who claims her life mate did come to the door; she married the man who repaired her furnace. But it is incalculably rare to find your partner waiting on your doorstep.

Rule 1. Talk to Everyone
Don't be embarrassed to let people know you are single. Be proud of it! You don't have to slither around in sack-cloth-and-ashes. Let everybody know that you are looking to meet that special someone and who knows? One of your friends, relatives or acquaintances might match you up with your everlasting love.

Rule 2: You Are in Control
You are in control of whom you decide to date and whether you see that person again. Yet all single people tend to think the other person holds all the cards. Dating is a wide open field these days. If two people exchange business cards or phone numbers, it is not etched in stone who should call whom first. If you are a woman waiting for the man to call, spring a surprise by calling him first. At least you will find out if the interest is mutual. And if you do take the initiative and get turned down, praise yourself for having made the effort to test the waters, then move on.

Dating is not a crap shoot. You make the choice as to whom you want to date and when. You don't have to go out with everyone you meet. If you just don't like someone well enough to date that person, tell the individual up front you are not interested in a relationship but you appreciate his or her interest in you. Never overlook the possibility of a friendship or business connection; you never know what can develop down the road.

Rule 3: Everything is Negotiable
Just because you may want to fall in love with someone who has the same passions as you, don't restrict yourself too much. Remember that everything is negotiable in life and in love.

If you meet someone you like who doesn't share your lifestyle, be open to learning from each other. Compromises can be reached if you care enough to explore the possibilities. One thing I have learned is that couples can be very creative together when they want to find solutions to the problems that crop up.

Just because you want to fall in love with someone who has a passion for boating and you meet someone who has a passion for horse riding doesn't mean you can't spend one weekend on the ocean and the next on a ranch. You can create a win-win situation. Similarly, if he's a steak and potatoes person, and you're a vegetarian, be open to exploring and learning from each other. Compromises can always be reached if you care enough to explore the possibilities.

Rule 4: Don't turn anything down before it is offered.

Don't rate a person on your first meeting. And don't say to yourself, "I won't see him/her again because _____!" Even if your instincts are right, the relationship could still blossom or you could meet your everlasting love through this person. I cannot stress this rule enough. In the rat race of life, we jump to conclusions about people without really knowing them. I have seen more potentially good relationships bite the dust before they even got off the ground.

Don't assume you know everything about a person on that first meeting, either. Even if you don't like what you see or hear on that first date, attune yourself to what you do like and see if more is there. Ebony is a middle-aged woman who has been married twice and "hurt too many times" as she puts it. But she keeps herself in the dating game because she strongly believes in the power of love. "I met three men I liked in one month," Ebony said. "One of them had a lot to offer me, he was good to me, and I really liked him. But he was so boring. And he's a big man, and I just don't care for large men. After a couple of dates, I knew I could not be with him. My friends encouraged me to give him more of a chance. I'm glad I got to know him better anyway. We give business referrals to each other; that seems to be what we have most in common. I know people who are good clients for him, and vice versa. We're helping each other out. And you know what? He's growing on me a little more now that I've known him longer. We still go out on occasion."

"Tenderness and kindness are not signs of weakness and despair but manifestations of strength and resolution."
Kahlil Gibran

STEP 9
Evaluating Your Dating Expectations

"Hatred paralyzes life; love releases it.
Hatred confuses life; love harmonizes it.
Hatred darkens life; love illumines it."

Martin Luther King, Jr.

Step 9: Avoid Negative Self-Fulfilling Prophecies.
You Will Attract What You Believe.

What are some of the self-fulfilling prophecies that you have told yourself before going on a date?

Have you ever said:
> They won't like me...
> We won't have anything in common...
> I don't know how to act on a date...
> I hate dating...

Now let's re-frame all those negative thoughts.
> I'm just going to be myself on a date...
> I know we'll have something in common...
> I'm going to have a great time tonight...
> Dating is fun...

Below you will find important dating etiquette that can often make the difference between making a connection or blowing an opportunity.

Don't: Talk about anything negative such as family or health problems. Don't talk about your financial status and never talk about past relationships, especially if they were bad.

Do: Talk about your goals, work, hobbies, favorite places, and your personal philosophies, Ask a lot of questions.

EXERCISES
STEP 9

Exercise #1: **Dating.** How do you want to feel when you're on a date with someone? Example: Secure, appreciated, respected, desired, etc.

_____

_____

Exercise #2: **Expectations.** What are your first-date expectations? (Examples: Friendship, Romance, Good Conversation, A Kiss, etc.)

_____

_____

Exercise #3: **Negative attitudes.** List the negative attitudes — self-fulfilling prophecies — that you've had towards dating? (Examples: "I'm never going to fall in love, I'm not attractive or smart enough, They won't be my type," etc.)

_____

_____

Exercise #4: **Affirmations.** Reframe these negatives into affirmations so you create a more favorable atmosphere for meeting and dating others. (Example: "Tonight I'm going to meet someone special. I know we'll have something in common.")

_____

_____

Exercise #5: **Surprises.** What kind of surprises would you give your date?

_____

_____

_____

Exercise #6: **More Surprises.** What kind of surprises would you like to get from your date?

_____

_____

Use space below for additional notes.

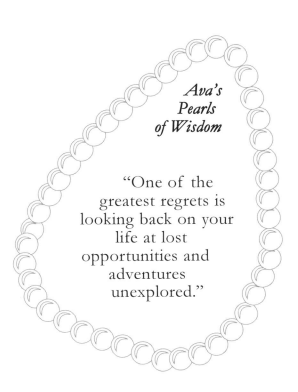

*Ava's
Pearls
of Wisdom*

"One of the greatest regrets is looking back on your life at lost opportunities and adventures unexplored."

Worksheet Week Three ~ Monday:

Continue self-image enhancement each morning, reinforcing this by saying positive affirmations. Repeat the affirmations 10 times throughout the day.

_____

_____

List more positive things you can bring to a relationship.

_____

_____

_____

List the people I saw today who most closely fit the description in my "personal profile".

_____

_____

_____

What I did to approach that person:

_____

_____

_____

What did I do today that made me more confident with others?

_____

_____

_____

Who did I ask out on a date? Did he/she accept? If so, how did it go? If not, why do I think he/she refused?

_____

_____

_____

What have I learned about myself and others?

_____

_____

What forms of self-improvement did I accomplish today?

_____

_____

_____

_____

_____

Describe the events of the day. Make observations of my behavior as well as that of others in the social activities I have participated in.

_____

_____

_____

_____

_____

_____

_____

_____

_____

_____

_____

_____

_____

_____

_____

Worksheet Week Three ~ Tuesday:

Continue self-image enhancement each morning, reinforcing this by saying positive affirmations. Repeat the affirmations 10 times throughout the day.

_____

My current dating philosophy is:

_____

_____

The most memorable thing that happened today was:

_____

_____

_____

My mind was occupied with thoughts of the following people:

_____

_____

_____

Today would have been better if:

_____

_____

_____

Who did I ask out on a date? Did he/she accept? If so, how did it go? If not, why do I think he/she refused?

_____

_____

_____

_____

What have I learned about myself and others?

_____

_____

_____

What types of self-improvement did I accomplish today?

_____

_____

_____

Did I spend more time being alone or with people? Which was most satisfying and why?

_____

_____

_____

_____

Describe the events of the day. Make observations of my behavior as well as that of others in the social activities I have participated in.

_____

_____

_____

_____

_____

_____

_____

Worksheet Week Three ~ Wednesday:

Continue self-image enhancement each morning, reinforcing this by saying positive affirmations. Repeat the affirmations 10 times throughout the day.

_____

My favorite time of day was: because:

_____

_____

The following best describes my feelings today (Use the emotional barometer):

_____

If I could change anything about today, it would be:

_____

_____

I felt powerful today when:

_____

_____

The person who most influenced me today was:

_____

_____

The most valuable lesson I learned today was:

_____

_____

What types of self-improvement did I accomplish today?

_____

_____

Did I spend more time being appreciative or critical of myself? What did I feel?

_____

_____

_____

_____

Describe the events of the day. Make observations of my behavior as well as that of others in the social activities I have participated in.

_____

_____

_____

_____

_____

_____

_____

_____

_____

_____

_____

_____

_____

Worksheet Week Three ~ Thursday:

Continue self-image enhancement each morning, reinforcing this by saying positive affirmations. Repeat the affirmations 10 times throughout the day.

Today I wish I had been:

_____

_____

The person I was most attracted to today was:

_____

_____

_____

What I did to approach that person:

_____

_____

What did I do today that made me more confident with others?

_____

_____

I was irritated today when:

_____

_____

_____

What have I learned about myself and others?

_____

_____

What types of self-improvement did I accomplish today?

_____

_____

Did I try to hide negative parts of my personality? If so, what were they? Why?

_____

_____

_____

_____

_____

Describe the events of the day. Make observations of my behavior as well as that of others in the social activities I have participated in.

_____

_____

_____

_____

_____

_____

_____

_____

_____

_____

_____

_____

_____

Worksheet Week Three ~ Friday:

Continue self-image enhancement each morning, reinforcing this by saying positive affirmations. Repeat the affirmations 10 times throughout the day.

_____

The best thing I did today was:

_____

_____

_____

List the people I saw today who most closely fit the description in my "personal profile".

_____

_____

_____

What I did to approach that person:

_____

_____

_____

What did I do today that made me more confident with others?

_____

_____

_____

Who did I ask out on a date? Did he/she accept? If so, how did it go? If not, why do I think he/she refused?

_____

_____

_____

_____

What have I learned about myself and others?

_____

_____

What types of self-improvement did I accomplish today?

_____

_____

Did I spend more time being appreciative or critical of others? What did I feel?

_____

_____

_____

_____

_____

Describe the events of the day. Make observations of my behavior as well as that of others in the social activities I have participated in.

_____

_____

_____

_____

_____

_____

_____

_____

_____

_____

_____

Worksheet Week Three ~ Saturday:

Continue self-image enhancement each morning, reinforcing this by saying positive affirmations. Repeat the affirmations 10 times throughout the day.

I think I impressed someone today when I:

_____

_____

_____

Today was a good day because:

_____

_____

_____

The person that I saw today that was most like me was:

_____

_____

_____

If I could eliminate one experience from today it would be:

_____

_____

_____

If there was one question I could have asked someone today, it would have been:

_____

_____

_____

What have I learned about myself and others?

_____

_____

_____

What types of self-improvement did I accomplish today?

_____

_____

What obstacles did I overcome this week? How did I accomplish them?

_____

_____

_____

_____

_____

_____

Describe the events of the day. Make observations of my behavior as well as that of others in the social activities I have participated in.

_____

_____

_____

_____

_____

_____

_____

_____

_____

_____

_____

Worksheet Week Three ~ Sunday:

Continue self-image enhancement each morning, reinforcing this by saying positive affirmations. Repeat the affirmations 10 times throughout the day.

It would have been a relief for me if I could have only:

_____

_____

The funniest thing that happened today was:

_____

_____

_____

My biggest obstacle today was:

_____

_____

I wish I had been more:

_____

_____

_____

The person that I would have liked to spend more time with was:

_____

_____

What have I learned about myself and others?

_____

_____

_____

What types of self-improvement did I accomplish today?

_____

_____

What emotions motivated the events of my week? Did I end the week with more positive or negative feeling? How do I plan to change the negative into positive?

_____

_____

_____

_____

_____

_____

Describe the events of the day. Make observations of my behavior as well as that of others in the social activities I have participated in.

_____

_____

_____

_____

_____

_____

_____

_____

_____

_____

_____

At the End of Week Three:

Review Steps 1-9. And pay particular attention to Steps 10, 11 and 12 as you enter the critical fourth and final week of the 30-Day Plan-of-Action for Everlasting Love.

Summarize how you feel about yourself at the end of this, the third week of the program. Include what you feel you have gained with respect to the thoughts and actions of others. What have you learned about yourself? What attributes have you observed in others that you made part of your personal behavior? What attributes have you discovered you would like in a partner?

_____

_____

_____

_____

_____

_____

_____

_____

_____

_____

_____

_____

_____

_____

_____

_____

_____

WEEK FOUR

Keeping Everlasting Love

"Life is a journey and love is what makes that journey worthwhile."
Ava Cadell

Steps 10 through 12 are all about keeping everlasting love

If you have not found your everlasting love yet, do no be discouraged. Continue to read the workbook and imagine that you are with the partner of your dreams. Visualize meeting your partner as if it were a movie. Your subconscious brain will understand this effectively. Use all your senses including sounds and colors. Dare to dream and really feel the various emotions as your visualize this movie from beginning to end. Of course make sure it has a happy, win-win conclusion for everyone. Now put a believable target date on your goal. Creative visualization is very powerful, so don't underestimate the power of suggestion.
Conceive it, believe it, and you will achieve it!

Be sure to note your various reactions and feelings in the given situations. After doing these exercises, you will be even more prepared when you find your everlasting love.

"Grow old with me!
The best is yet to be."
Robert Browning to
Elizabeth Barrett Browning

Instructions

Week Four ~ KEEPING EVERLASTING LOVE

Step 10: Making Your Partner Feel Good
Step 11: How to Fulfill Your Lover's Sexual Needs
Step 12: Committing Yourself to Everlasting Love

Week Four Instructions:

Steps 10-12
This the final week in Dr. Ava's 30-Day Plan-of-Action.

~NEW~ projects during Week Four:

♥ This is the week that demands dedication to your social time commitment. Arrange your social schedule first! Give yourself two free evenings this week.

♥ With renewed vigor, and buoyed by the self-confidence and insight of your recent experiences, include even more social activities in your schedule which, in the past, were uncomfortable or unpleasant. Go forward into the challenge. Once again, you will see that you are able to handle these situations differently.

♥ Extend invitations to others to join you in social activities. Be open to all reciprocal invitations from others.

♥ Attend a seminar, lecture or workshop on a subject that interests you.

♥ Plan A: Give a seminar/workshop or lecture on your favorite subject or hobby. You will feel confident speaking about a subject with which you are familiar. People will look up to you. Invite your friends and business associates. Emphasize that they bring their friends and associates. Make the meeting into a mixer for all invited, especially for you

(e.g. give a talk about cooking for singles, romantic poetry, staying in shape, computer software, playing a musical instrument, humor, art, money, spirituality, wine, stargazing, etc.)

♥ Plan B: Host a party that is purely social in context, to celebrate your completion of the 30-Day Plan-of-Action for the 12 Steps to Everlasting Love. Again, make sure you ask the people you invite to include their friends. The more people-mixing, the better.

♥ Ask out someone you have been admiring from afar. Be persistent in your overtures, especially if you haven't yet found that individual who might just be your "everlasting love".

♥ As before, if rejected, have the strength to move onward. It is their loss, not yours. Rejoice in your ability to stay focused on your purpose. Each rejection is a step closer to success. You are no longer the person you were when you started this program.

"If love makes the world go around then sex keeps it on course."

Dr. Ava Cadell

Intimate Communication

Things to Remember

♥ Always communicate your wants and needs positively.

♥ Share words of appreciation.

♥ Compliment your partner's physical and mental attributes.

♥ Show interest in your partner's feelings.

♥ Use a tone of voice that displays a romantic sentiment.

Things to Avoid

♥ Never rate or underestimate your partner's intelligence.

♥ Don't blame your partner for a lack of creativity.

♥ Don't criticize your partner in public.

♥ Don't talk about problems or anything negative during a date.

♥ Never compare your partner to a former lover.

♥ Don't say anything you know you will regret later.

As your relationship progresses, there are certain action steps that may help you strengthen the dialogue between you and your partner. Be creative and add other ideas to the suggestions below:

Things to Encourage

♥ Talk about yourself openly and encourage your partner to do the same.

♥ Ask your partner what would be their perfect date and why.

♥ Verbalize your appreciation for what you like about your partner.

♥ Make a wish list of three things you would like to experience and ask your partner to do the same.

♥ Spend an evening discussing each other's list.

♥ After a date, call or send a note or fax expressing your appreciation, indicating you had a good time.

Always follow up every date and relationship encounter with a personal reflection and review of what was said, what took place and, most importantly, how you felt. If applicable, what you would have done differently.

STEP TEN
Making Your Partner Feel Good About Her/Himself

"Sex is as important as eating or drinking,
and we ought to allow
the one appetite
to be satisfied
with as little false modesty
as the other."

Marquis de Sade

Step 10: Recognize Your Partner's Attributes
and Incorporate Them into Words and Actions.

The number one reason that someone will choose to date you over anyone else is simply because you make them feel good when they're around you.

Think of all the songs about feeling good: James Brown's "I Feel Good," Aretha Franklin's "You Make Me Feel Like A Natural Woman," The Beatles line "You Make Me Feel So Fine," from "Hard Days Night", and Dr. Feel Good's "When Someone Makes You Feel Good, You Want To Sing About It."

Once you think you've found everlasting love, don't take it for granted. Continue to compliment your partner both physically and emotionally. Let them know they are making a difference in your life. Continue to be supportive and interested in what they're doing. Never lose your curiosity.

Set goals in all aspects of your life together including social, educational, romantic, spiritual, professional even financial. Remember to exchange little gifts for no special reason, discuss dream vacations, career goals and even new hobbies you can share. Re-live peak moments from when you first met by going to some of the same places, look at old photos or videos and continue to express appreciation for each other.

Do you already know if your partner is primarily a visual person? Or is he/she a kinesthetic or auditory person?

"Good communication is like learning to Tango.
Two people communicating with their minds and their bodies responding to one another,"

Dr. Ava Cadell

EXERCISES
STEP 10

Exercise #1: **Modalities.** Statistics show that 40% of the population is visual, 40% is kinesthetic and 20% is auditory. Most people combine two out of three modalities. Which one do you resonate with the most? What do you think is your partner's primary system? Which one are you most attracted to?

1. I Am: _____

2. I am attracted to: _____

3. My partner is: _____

Exercise #2: **Compliments.** If you have a partner, a prospect, or someone you're dating, list five compliments you can give them. Examples: "I love being with you", "I love your sense of humor", "I really appreciate your kindness", "You make me feel good", etc.

_____

_____

_____

_____

Exercise #3: **Compliments, Take 2.** List five compliments you'd like to receive from a mate.

_____

_____

_____

_____

_____

_____

_____

Exercise #4: **Praise.** Praise is the most effective commodity on earth. Everyone loves to be validated, and it is absolutely the best way to create rapport with everyone in your world — your mate, family members, fellow workers, the bus driver, etc. Find a way to praise at least three people a day. It will make you and others feel good. List some examples of praise you would give others.

_____

_____

_____

_____

Exercise #5: **Praise Yourself.** What do you think people would praise about you? Give three examples.

_____

_____

Exercise #6: **Not Me!** What do you think people would never say about you? Give three examples.

_____

_____

Use the space below for additional notes.

STEP ELEVEN
How To Fulfill Your Lover's Sexual Needs

*"Sex and beauty are inseparable, like life and consciousness.
And the intelligence which goes with sex and beauty,
and arises out of sex and beauty is intuition."*
David Herbert Lawrence

Much Ado About Sex

"Sex appeal is the keynote of our civilizations"
Henri Bergson

The purpose and meaning of sex has intrigued and mystified us through the ages. Various societies have wrestled with or "coped" with the power of sex in myriad ways. Far Eastern cultures regarded sex as a mystical ritual to achieve union with God. On the other hand, the decline of the Roman Empire was preceded by sexual debasement and demoralization - a complete dissociation from spirituality. Some Middle Eastern and Victorian British and American traditions have hidden sex in the closet and underneath untold yards of unnecessary clothing. Many ancient African mores perceived sex as a rite-of-passage into adulthood, a mating ritual. Some societies go around it, some view it as a "problem" and pass it on down to the next generation to deal with, and a few revel in its glory and ecstasy.

What sex is: Sex is a precious gift to someone who is worthy to receive it. Our sexual gifts are as valuable as any other part of ourselves that we prize. Selecting the right sexual partner to give to, and receiving from the right partner, is as important a decision as choosing anything you place a high value upon. Sex has many beautiful qualities that we are coming to appreciate. In this era of "natural ingredients", sex is a natural "high", perhaps even the best of nature's uplifts. It can energize us and make us feel more creative afterward. Sex is a wonderful form of self-expression, infinitely artistic. We don't often think about this, but sex is an affirmation of self-confidence and self-love.

And sex can heal. Sex can renew stamina, not deplete it. It can free us from emotional wounds that have been buried deep in our body tissues, much like the experience of "Rolfing", only sex is unforced. (Rolfing became popular about 20 years ago as a deep-tissue massage therapy. It releases painful emotions that have become lodged in the muscles and caused stiffness from tension.) Sex has so many forms of expression. It is both beautiful and erotic. It is gentle and assertive. It is relaxing and energizing. But most of all, it is a unique connection to all of life - it is spiritual, mental, emotional, physical. Sex is truly a divine pleasure.

What sex is not: It is equally important in defining sex to weed out what doesn't belong in its repertoire of images. Because "sex sells" in the marketplace and in the advertisements that bombard us daily, we are prone to confuse sex with many things which it is not. And we are equally apt to confuse sex with its ignorant definitions of the past which kept us from its hidden pleasures. First and foremost, sex is not a sin. It didn't make it to the Top 10 commandments, so it must be okay! Besides, how could anything that creates new life be an affront to God, when life is God-given. Sex is also not dirty; it is not something of which to be ashamed, like leprosy. And it is not unhealthy as long as proper protection is used. Sex won't make you go blind or go crazy. In fact, sexual fitness can improve your health, not take away from it. Sex is not perverted or unnatural. Love-making between consenting adults is their private matter, and as long as it doesn't hurt anyone, it does not defy the laws of nature.

Sex is not to be misused as a weapon. Withholding sex to punish a partner is a sign of poor communication and stored-up anger; and it does not give power to the "withholder". To the other extreme, forcing one's self sexually on another person is a sign of inadequacy, not power or real strength.

Sex is not a healthy addiction. A sexual addiction or compulsion is an escape from love. Sex is also not a sport; it is not merely a form of exercise. It is a body function, yes, but its many pleasures are not achieved by experiencing a body part. Besides, using sex as an impersonal exercise is ultimately not fulfilling, either sexually or emotionally.

Sex is not just intercourse or oral copulation; as we know about anything in life, "the journey is as important as the destination". Sex is not love, but is often confused with love. How many times have you heard someone say in jest "I'm in lust!". It isn't as funny as the joke is meant to be. Is such a person afraid to go the next step and fall in love? Commitment makes the sex grow deeper, but having sex for its own sake is not everlasting love.

Self-Love: What do you think is the most common, universal sexual issue? No, it isn't penis or breast size, but it is the attitude looming behind your physical attributes that counts more than what you look like. And that manifests itself by causing us to feel inhibited. Inhibition begins with that old bugaboo "lack of self-worth".

Anyone who grew up on this planet has experienced this loss of self-esteem and self-value. It has many causes, from family conflicts to society's ills. What matters now is giving yourself a positive self-perception. You've earned it. You deserve it. Lack of self-worth isn't an item that stands alone like a crooked nose or big feet. Our self-worth affects every area of our lives across the board. It's an awful thing to feel. In fact, often we run from feeling it and its shame-based origins. We overeat, overindulge, overspend - anything to keep from feeling bad about ourselves. A lack of self-worth can cause us to spiral down into the pits before we realize what's happening. As one man once said to me: "I can sure dig myself into a hole with very little effort". Self-esteem affects one's confidence, ability to have positive relationships, career success, self-assertion and self-expression. Low self-worth can stop us in our tracks and keep us petrified of experiencing life and its myriad pleasures.

Everyone is inhibited about something, whether it is physical appearance, performance as a lover or the ability to let go and have an incredible orgasm with their partner. Some people are so inhibited about sex they have never explored their bodies to discover their erogenous zones. And if they don't know what arouses them, they surely cannot communicate it to a partner. Statistics show that over 78% of women have never explored the inside of their vagina. This is sad, because knowledge equals power. It's imperative to be aware when your body is feeling different, especially when it comes to examining the breasts for possible lumps. I would like to encourage women to feel the inside of their body, probe and get to know their cervix, learn to recognize when they are ovulating and note any changes in bodily stimulation and emotions. Women need to familiarize themselves with bodily secretions, as well, and what they mean.

Self-pleasuring is a good tool for utilizing fantasy to overcome inhibitions. In fact, there are many good reasons for pleasuring one's self. It feels good. You can explore your own sexual response patterns. You can enjoy sex without feeling desperate for a partner. You can relieve tensions. For women, you can relieve pelvic congestion, especially during menstruation. Masturbation is also an excellent way to reenter into sexual activity after a heart attack or other medical problem. People who feel good about pleasuring themselves are much less likely to have sexual problems. If you take responsibility for your sexual needs and responses, you are likely to make a good sexual adjustment. Let's take a look at some of the self-pleasuring myths and realities.

Self-Pleasuring Myths
- Self-pleasuring causes insanity, headaches, blindness, nosebleeds, nymphomania and warts.
- Too much self-pleasuring is harmful.
- Self-pleasuring is unnatural.
- Pleasuring yourself is immature.
- Self-pleasuring is for simple-minded people.
- Self-pleasuring is a substitute for sexual intercourse.
- Self-pleasuring is socially unacceptable.
- You may begin to prefer self-pleasuring to intercourse.

Self-Pleasuring Realities

♥ No evidence exists that self-pleasuring causes physical or mental problems.

♥ It is a healthy way to take responsibility for your own orgasm.

♥ It is an excellent way to learn about your sexual responses so you can share them with your partner.

♥ Intercourse with a partner and self-pleasuring are complementary sexual experiences.

♥ Many sexually active people who have available partners still enjoy self-pleasuring.

Far from being an "unnatural" act, self-pleasuring is a very natural function. It is healthy both psychologically and physiologically. And there is no "normal" rate associated with self-pleasuring; frequency varies enormously from one person to the next. Some people fantasize while pleasuring themselves, others don't.

And there is no "right" or "best" way to have an orgasm or to masturbate. Some people reach a climax quietly while pleasuring themselves; others thrash about and make a lot of noise. These aspects vary greatly, and are not judgmental criteria.

It is also natural for children to masturbate out of curiosity and for pleasure. Guilt results only when a child is told by others that self-pleasuring is wrong. It is important for parents to become as well informed about sex as possible, so we can all convey healthy sexual values to our children, clearly and effectively.

Self-pleasuring offers a great exercise in overcoming inhibitions. Looking at your genitals as you masturbate (either directly or in a mirror can help you to notice the different parts as they really are, rather than how textbooks portray them. It will also help you to gain self-acceptance about your body and how it functions sexually.

In a relationship, self-pleasuring takes the pressure off the partner to perform at times of stress or during a temporary change in lifestyle. Even in the best of unions, sexual tastes can vary and one partner may need more activity than another. Self-pleasuring can provide a healthy release between love-making sessions when both partners are desirous of sex.

Self-love and self-pleasuring are the first natural steps to a healthy sexuality. It is so vital to develop a loving, patient and understanding attitude toward one's self, and to learn to pleasure one's self, so each of us can bring that knowledge and caring into a union with our everlasting love.

Male Sexuality. Men have been taught to rigidly conform to cultural myths about themselves and their sexuality. If they don't live up to those myths, they incur much guilt and negative feelings. As cartoonist Dan O'Neill once said in jest, "In the beginning, God created man...and his penis." Men worry unnecessarily about the size of their penis, when in fact the size of a man's heart is much more important to a woman. If men have difficulty in achieving the standards of maleness, they have been told to remain silent and bear the load. The limits imposed by these unrealistic standards have inhibited men from exploring and fulfilling the total range of sexual options. Below is a list of unhealthy myths and societal messages men get:

DO:	perform, get it up, keep it up, achieve, always be turned on, be a sex machine, control, have sex only with young attractive women, give women orgasms, have a big penis, hide your feelings of fear, inadequacy, rejection or helplessness.

DON'T:	quit, fail, feel, be vulnerable, be weak, be receptive, be passive, take responsibility for birth control.

The above DO's and DON'Ts are not attractive to women, so why must they be perpetuated on men? To achieve a full and satisfying sex life, men need what women need: self-knowledge, facts, options, techniques and honesty. The two genders are not so different in their basic wants and desires.

Female Sexuality. The confusing sexual messages women get from society's projected attitudes are equally as damaging, if not more so. During childhood and adolescence, women are often taught to fear sex, which manifests in the following:

DON'T:	touch "down there", talk about sex, learn about sex, read about sex, get turned on, give in to sexual desire, be available, kiss on the first date, feel sexual, be too forward.

However, women are expected to hide their womanly wiles behind an attractive, mannequin-like pose and do the following:

DO:	be attractive, be obedient, be passive, be sensitive, be loving, be nurturing, maintain a "good" reputation, wait for the male to initiate, expect the man to know all about sex, refuse a man when he asks you to be sexual.

As if these weren't enough, women are bombarded with other cultural messages as well:

- ♥ Sex is only for men's pleasure and for making babies
- ♥ You aren't allowed to have sex until you're married.
- ♥ You should only have sex with men.
- ♥ Your only goal is to please your man.
- ♥ You should only share love with one person during your life.
- ♥ Sex is dirty; sexual desires are bad.
- ♥ Only the missionary position is right; any other sexual position is kinky.
- ♥ You must not have sex during your period.
- ♥ Never reveal that you are sexually experienced, even if you are.
- ♥ Fake your orgasm, if you can't reach one.
- ♥ Your naked body is shameful and embarrassing.
- ♥ Women shouldn't be too successful, especially in sex.
- ♥ You aren't doing it correctly until you have a "vaginal" orgasm. (This is attributed to Sigmund Freud, who said that women have two kinds of orgasm: 1. clitoral, which is immature, and 2. vaginal, from penile thrusting, which is the "right", mature kind of orgasm.)
- ♥ It is selfish and demanding to want clitoral stimulation.
- ♥ Foreplay isn't necessary because intercourse is the goal of sex.
- ♥ You must have a perfect, "hourglass" figure.
- ♥ You should always be naturally lubricated.
- ♥ Birth control is the woman's responsibility.
- ♥ You must have sex when your partner demands it, not when you want it.
- ♥ You must climax together.
- ♥ You need a man to be whole.

Can all of these sweeping statements be true? If our genitals are as valuable as priceless rubies, why are they spoken of as "dirty"? If sex is so beautiful, why do people shame it? If sex is a no-no before marriage, then how can we be expected to perform perfectly and know everything about it on the wedding night?

It is no wonder that women are often as confused as men about sex; feel guilty, alone and worried; are uncomfortable with their bodies; are waiting for IT to happen; are masturbating in secret, if at all; and are worried about whether their genitals smell and taste normal.

Society's messages are obviously ignorant, and have been handed down to us from times when people just didn't deal with "such matters". It is up to each woman to establish her own sexual values, and overcome the taboos with self-knowledge, creating options, being honest with herself and others, knowing the facts, learning techniques, and sharing her needs with others.

The clitoris was designed to open sexual doors for women, literally. The very word, "clitoris", derives from the Greek word for "key", as in the key to female sexuality. It opens women up to pleasure. And for a woman to revel in and thoroughly enjoy sex, her mind must be in the right place and not constantly fighting the negative messages above. The clitoris has its own rhythm and will not be rushed. A woman must have a connection from her brain, and the fantasies it activates, to her clitoris; thereby taking responsibility for her own satisfaction. If her mind is in harmony with her clitoris, she is moving with her own sexual rhythm.

Safe Sex: Ironically, our sexual knowledge is expanding at a time in which there is extreme concern about sexually transmitted diseases. As much as we may desire to experiment and free ourselves of sexual taboos, it is equally important to be sexually responsible, both to ourselves and others. AIDS, caused by infection with the Human Immunodeficiency Virus (HIV) is considered the most serious health crisis of the century. More than 30 million people worldwide are now living with the AIDS virus, and about 16,000 new victims are infected every day. To date, it has no cure. If you get it, not only will your sex life be over, so will the rest of your life. We must also be equally cautious about other known sexual diseases such as syphilis, gonorrhea chlamydia, genital herpes and warts, and trichomonas. Even though treatable, these latter two can cause serious health problems.

The "sexual revolution" is not over, because each generation is showing more eagerness to explore healthy sexuality. This is no time to retreat from sexual expression, but rather to become as responsible about it as you would if you were learning mountain climbing. All over the world, people are protecting their health by using erotic sexual techniques that prevent or greatly reduce the possibility of infection. Some of these include tasty condoms, spermicide and gels for oral pleasures.

A "safe sex" approach to lovemaking means finding ways to remain uninfected no matter what your sexual lifestyle may be. It is not a time to crawl back into the closet and wait for the "sexual crisis" to be over. However, it is a wonderful time to explore the joys of monogamy and growing more deeply close to one partner. Couples may enjoy exploring ways to keep a closed relationship vital and adventurous while protecting their sexual health.

For those who are sexually active and not monogamous, there are many techniques such as mutual self-pleasuring and "outer course" as different from "intercourse". These include flirting, communicating, cuddling, tender kissing and massaging. The most important thing to remember is to avoid the exchange of bodily fluids, and that the most erotic organ is the brain!

Achieving the ultimate through sex: I like to believe that in the new millennium sex will rise to new heights as a healing energy between partners. Many ancient cultures knew well the tremendous power of sex when combined with love. Perhaps we should look to that ancient advice in creating our future views of sex as an ultimate pleasure in partnerships. What were the great mystics trying to tell us about sex and spiritual union? Sexual ecstasy with our "soul mate" is the attunement with our life force that we all wish to find. How many single people place ads that read, "I'm looking for my soul mate"? Deep down inside we wish for that comfort in spiritual, mental, emotional and physical closeness with another, and sex is one of the most binding aspects of it. What is the ultimate in sex but a glistening sense of self-worth and self-love afterward? We feel we can conquer the world when our home fires are burning!

As we grow healthier in our body and mind, our sexual selves will grow too. And that can refurbish and replenish our desires, renew our strengths and minimize our weaknesses. Sex can, and should, be discussed without judgment. A healthy attitude toward sex, free from guilt and secrecy, and a hearty body, a curious mind and a happy heart will open up new sexual vistas for the human race in the decades to come.

"If you just set people in motion they'll heal themselves."
Roth Gabrielle

Turn-Ons & Turn-Offs

Women's Turn-Ons!

Men's Turn-Ons!

Women's Turn-Ons	Men's Turn-Ons
Self-Confident Men	Women Who Communicate Openly
Men Who Are Good Listeners	Women Who Take the Initiative
Sensitive Men	Adventuresome Women
Men Who Set the Mood for Romance	Affectionate Women
Men Who Put Their Woman Before Business	Women Who Create Romantic Memories
Men Who Like To Cuddle	Women Who Are Uninhibited
A Man With a Slow Hand	Women Who Wear Sexy Lingerie
Men Who Are Unselfish Lovers	Women Who Are Responsive
Men Who Communicate Before -AND- After Sex	Women Who Enjoy Erotic Dialogue
Men Who Show Their Gratitude	Women Who Show Their Appreciation
Men With a Little-Boy Quality	Women With a Good Sense of Humor
Even-Tempered Men	Easy-Going Women

Universal Turn Offs!

Not Romantic	Inconsiderate	Too Aggressive
Poor Grooming	Incessant Braggart	Not Adventurous
Lack of Humor	Too Unreliable	Overly Critical
Poor Hygiene	Excessive Complaining	Low Self-Esteem
	Overly Sensitive	

12 Steps to Great Sex

<u>Number One - Flirt.</u> Flirting is an art which instills sexual confidence. It can be a subtle glance or a purposeful squeeze, but the goal of flirting is to set the stage for romance and create sexual anticipation.

<u>Number Two - Kiss.</u> Make kissing a ritual at least twice a day for 12 seconds in the morning and at night and kiss your lover passionately.

<u>Number Three - Communicate.</u> When communication is great, the sex is great too. Don't neglect to tell your partner all the things you love most about him/her. Express your appreciation for each other physically, intellectually and emotionally. Exchange a wish list of three things that you think may heighten a sexual experience for you.

<u>Number Four - Stimulate All 5 Senses.</u> If you don't use just one of your five senses during lovemaking, you are missing out on 20% of pleasure. Take the time to prepare something to enhance each one of your senses prior to lovemaking. Surprise your taste buds with honey; turn a simple room into a romantic one with candlelight; play music that will get you and your lover in the mood for love; use a variety of lotions and oils to massage your lover slowly and sensuously; and finally, the sense of smell has been proven to be the basis for sexual attraction. You can wear your lover's favorite fragrance or adorn your room with scented candles, incense or flowers.

<u>Number Five - Discover Erogenous Zones.</u> The best way to find your lover's erogenous zones is to caress and kiss your lucky lover from head to toe, moving only half an inch at a time. Don't leave any area unmapped. Ask for your lover to rate his or her erogenous zones on a pleasure scale from 1 to 10. Now, it's time to trade places.

<u>Number Six - Synchronized Breathing.</u> When you are sexually excited, your breathing increases. Breathe in the essence of life and synchronized breathing is truly a sense of unity. As one person breathes in, the other person breathes out. This "meditation" can prepare a couple for the sexual journey ahead.

<u>Number Seven - Share Erotica.</u> Any form of erotica including videos, literature or magazines can provide a therapeutic value to couples wanting to learn more about sex. So whether you enjoy the bawdy tales of *Lady Chatterly's Lover* or the erotica of *Playboy*, sharing fantasies can embolden your love life or reenergize a stale relationship by adding sizzle and spice.

Number Eight - Oral Delights. First, we'll talk about *fellatio*, the sucking of the man's penis and most men will agree that, as a means to getting or restarting an erection, it is unparalleled. *Cunnilingus*, the art of kissing a woman's clitoris and vulva (visible external part of the vagina) is one of the most effective ways to bring a woman to climax.

Number Nine - Love Toys. You don't have to go outside your home to have a wide choice of love toys. Regular household items can be a great substitute. If you blindfold your partner with a scarf and comb a pasta spoon through his/her hair, it may feel like long, sensual fingernails. A gentle tap with a spatula or wooden spoon might be just what your partner desires. Don't forget to experiment with food!

Number Ten - Discover Her G-Spot. It is a fact that 78% of women do not explore the inside of their own bodies, yet the G-spot (I like to call it the Goddess Spot), located approximately 2 inches inside the opening to the vagina can bring about a longer, deeper, more powerful orgasm than a clitoral orgasm.

Number Eleven - Discover His H-Spot. Men also have a Hot-Spot, although I prefer to refer to it as the Hero-Spot which is the prostate gland. Some men say that their "H" spot is just a knuckle inside the anus and it can be effectively stimulated by the partner's insertion of her finger in a "come hither" motion.

Number Twelve - Make Love in Different Positions. Don't always make love in the same position, in the same place, at the same time because that's predictable. Make love standing up, side-by-side, woman-on-top, missionary or doggie-style. Do it in the bathroom, on the dining room table, over the kitchen sink, on the tumble dryer or on the staircase.

"Safe, loving sex is the best prescription for good health."
Ava Cadell

Step 11: Discover Your Partner's Needs, Wants and Desires Through Open Communication

If your everlasting love is taking his or her time showing up, do not give up hope. Continue on and finish the workbook to learn secrets that successful couples have mastered and you can use when your time comes.

On the other hand, if you have found someone that you believe is compatible mentally, physically, emotionally and spiritually, this is your opportunity to keep the flames of passion burning.

If you choose to have a sexual relationship before commitment or marriage, make sure you both discuss the options and the consequences of such a relationship. This decision must be bilateral so that no one feels pressured, guilty or obligated in any way. I am a firm believer that as long as two consentual adults agree to have sex because they both want to enjoy it, they are not hurting anyone and it feels good, then it's okay.

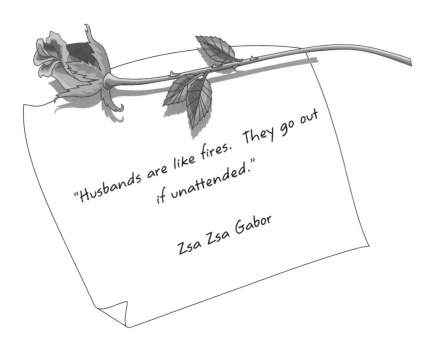

"Husbands are like fires. They go out if unattended."

Zsa Zsa Gabor

EXERCISES
STEP 11

Exercise #1: **Safer sex preferences.** Share with your partner the kinds of safe sex activities you like most: cuddling, kissing, phone sex, massaging, watching erotic movies, etc.

_____

_____

_____

Exercise #2: **Sexual likes and dislikes.** Initiate a conversation with your partner about your sexual preferences. How do you (and your partner) like your loving? For example do you like it: romantic, passionate, playful, dominating, submissive, experimental, wild?

_____

_____

_____

Exercise #3: **Ask for it.** Learn to ask for what you want. What kind of massage would you like from your partner? (hard, soft, slow?) Be specific and describe the perfect massage.

_____

_____

_____

Exercise #4: **Favorite sexual activities?** Make a list of at least ten sexual activities, then prioritize them in order of your level of arousal. For example: kissing, receiving oral sex, intercourse (woman on top), mutual masturbation, using sex toys, role playing...you get the picture. If you don't already know what turns you on, you won't be able to communicate your needs, wants and desires to your partner.

1. _____   6. _____

2. _____   7. _____

3. _____   8. _____

4. _____   9. _____

5. _____   10. _____

Exercise #5: **How do you feel?** After lovemaking, tell your partner how it made you feel. (I love the way your massage made me feel. You have the most beautiful touch. You're a fantastic kisser!)

_____

_____

Exercise #6: **Share a fantasy.** Begin to describe an exciting fantasy and let your partner end it. If it's acceptable to both of you, turn it into reality.

_____

_____

_____

_____

Use this space for additional notes.

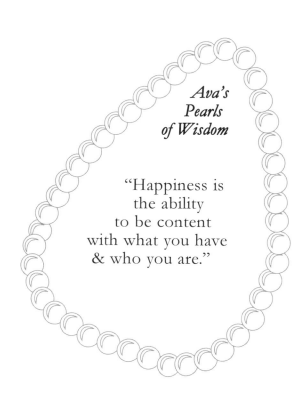

Ava's
Pearls
of Wisdom

"Happiness is
the ability
to be content
with what you have
& who you are."

STEP TWELVE

Committing Yourself to Everlasting Love

"There are never enough 'I love You's.'"

Lenny Bruce

Step 12: Abide by the Principles You Have Applied, Sustain Creativity, Respect, and Support.

Congratulations, you have stuck with your game plan and come so far. That in itself is a vital commitment. But, don't think that commitment is something you only need to know when you have a partner. Commitment applies to everything in life to which you are dedicated. So, go ahead and finish the last lap of the workbook whether you have found your soul mate or not. Then you'll be truly ready for everlasting love.

♥ How do you know when your partner is ready to make a commitment? Believe me, it's not just their words. It's a combination of what they say, what they do and what they convey with their body language. How can you find out if they're ready to commit?

1. Tell them how you feel about them and see what response you get.
2. Ask them if you will be spending special holidays together.
3. Ask them how they would feel if you started dating other people.
4. Ask where they see your relationship going over a period of one year.

♥ If they tell you what you want to hear, acknowledge what they said and let them know how happy it makes you feel. If they don't tell you what you want to hear, again, acknowledge and repeat it so that you understand. Then ask them what you can do, if anything, to improve your relationship.

"Selfish persons are incapable of loving others, but they are not capable of loving themselves either."

Eric Fromm

STEP TWELVE

COMMITTING YOURSELF TO EVERLASTING LOVE

"You gotta know when to hold 'em, know when to fold 'em."
Kenny Rogers

Like a high point in a card game, at this time you need to evaluate your relationship. Is it worth holding onto or should you let it go? Don't stay in it just because you think the relationship has potential. The good feelings must outweigh the bad.

Remember that you never really know someone until you have gone through some kind of trauma together, whether it's sickness, financial problems, family difficulties or anything else. There is no such thing as everlasting love without problems. As long as you continue to respect and trust each other, to stay creative (not predictable and boring), to feel mutual support through both good times and bad, your love will continue to grow and last until the end of time.

This is the 12th Step to Everlasting Love. If, by now, you feel you've found your true love, don't take your partner and this blessed possibility for granted. Nurture your union with praise, understanding and compassion. And know that everlasting love is not always fuzzy and warm. Any great relationship may leave you with character lines.

There are five stages to a good relationship: 1) Attraction 2) Falling in Love 3) Uncertainty 4) Commitment and 5) Falling Back in Love Again.

Without a doubt, the commitment stage is the most challenging. It's not that hard to fall in love, but it can be hard, hard work in the love-becomes-commitment stage. If you're still looking for Mr./Ms. Right, continue to follow the Steps. Incorporate them into your daily routine and you will find the perfect partner for you. Remember, like attracts like. Take on the qualities you want in a perfect mate, and it will be easier for your perfect mate to find you. What they don't tell you in the fairy tales is that Cinderella's glass slippers were killing her feet; Prince Charming suffered from indigestion and even Rapunzel had bad hair days. Everyone has an off day and nobody is perfect. But, they all lived happily ever after and so can you!

Conceive it, believe it and you will achieve it!

EXERCISES
STEP 12

Exercise #1: **Commitment.** Many relationships hit the wall when love becomes commitment. Ask yourself, "What is my level of commitment? (Am I committed to staying in a relationship as long as everything is easy and there are no problems? Is my commitment strong enough to weather the rough times?)" Write down your concerns and/or fear regarding commitment.

_____

_____

_____

_____

_____

Exercise #2: **Nurturing.** Once we've secured the partner of our dreams, the biggest mistake we make in our relationships is to quit doing the fun and exciting things that brought us together in the first place. Write down all the things you've been doing to nurture your relationship up until now. Continue doing them. Examples: Flirting with each other, giving surprise gifts, making phone calls just because you were thinking of your partner, etc.

_____

_____

_____

_____

Exercise #3: **Everlasting love.** Describe your ingredients for everlasting love. (Example: Friendship, respect, passion, trust, communication, etc.)

_____

_____

_____

_____

Exercise #4: Write down how you would like your lover to describe you.

_____

_____

_____

_____

Exercise #5: How would you like your partner to treat you? Be specific in all areas, including socially, sexually, emotionally and professionally.

_____

_____

_____

How well do you know your partner? Write down your partner's sexual turn-ons & turn-offs.

_____

_____

_____

Write down a physical, emotional & appreciative compliment you would like to receive.

_____

_____

_____

Use the space below for additional notes.

Ava's
Pearls
of Wisdom

"Every person
that we meet,
no matter
how briefly,
impacts our lives."

Worksheet Week Four ~ Monday:

The things I love about myself are:

_____

_____

_____

What I am grateful for today:

_____

_____

_____

How do I see my confidence building?

_____

_____

I believe I could heighten a romantic experience by:

_____

_____

_____

Today it was my choice to:

_____

_____

I believe I am getting better at:

_____

_____

Write down what I told my partner (or date) that I wanted today.

_____

_____

Write down what I wanted from my partner (or date) that I did not ask for.

_____

_____

_____

_____

Write down how you feel when you are with your partner. Use your emotional barometer and write down as many emotions as you want.

_____

_____

_____

_____

Use space below for additional notes:

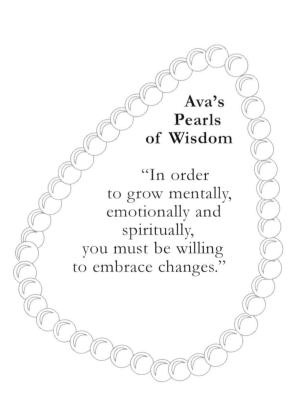

**Ava's
Pearls
of Wisdom**

"In order
to grow mentally,
emotionally and
spiritually,
you must be willing
to embrace changes."

Worksheet Week Four ~ Tuesday:

When I look in the mirror, my favorite physical features are:

_____

_____

The most enjoyable time of the day for me was? Because:

_____

_____

I felt most powerful today when: Because:

_____

_____

Today I wish I had taken a greater interest in:

_____

_____

What would I change about today's events if I could?

_____

_____

What surprises could I give my partner?

_____

_____

What additional things can I do to show how much I care?

_____

_____

Write down what I wanted from my partner (or date) that I did not ask for.

_____

_____

_____

What made me feel good today?

_____

_____

_____

Use space below for additional notes:

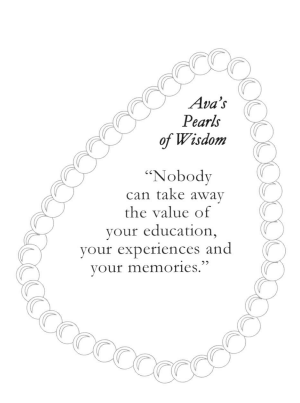

Ava's
Pearls
of Wisdom

"Nobody
can take away
the value of
your education,
your experiences and
your memories."

Worksheet Week Four ~ Wednesday:

Today was a good day because:

_____

_____

I am getting better at:

_____

_____

One thing I love about myself is: Because:

_____

_____

I wish I had spent more time with: Because:

_____

_____

I worry that:

_____

_____

My greatest joy today was:

_____

_____

Write down what I told my partner (or date) that I wanted today.

_____

_____

Write down what I wanted from my partner (or date) that I did not ask for.

_____

_____

_____

How did I implement positive changes to reach my goals?

_____

_____

_____

Use space below for additional notes:

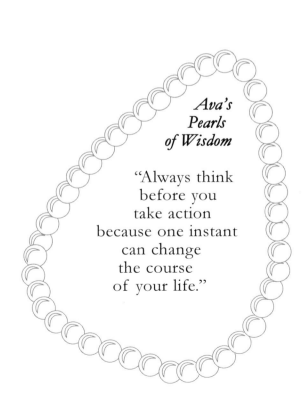

*Ava's
Pearls
of Wisdom*

"Always think
before you
take action
because one instant
can change
the course
of your life."

Worksheet Week Four ~ Thursday:

If my dreams come true, my relationship will:

_____

_____

_____

My favorite form of communication today was (e.g. talking, listening, writing, body language): Because:

_____

_____

_____

Select 3 positive and 2 negative words from the emotional barometer to describe your feelings today.

_____

_____

_____

Today I should have:

_____

_____

_____

Today I never should have:

_____

_____

_____

Today I felt most romantic when:

_____

_____

_____

_____

_____

Write down what I told my partner (or date) that I wanted today.

_____

_____

Write down what I wanted from my partner (or date) that I did not ask for.

_____

_____

_____

What behavior will I have to revoke in order to move forward?

_____

_____

_____

Use space below for additional notes:

Ava's
Pearls
of Wisdom

"No matter
how little
you have,
you can always
give the gift
of love, support
and comfort."

Worksheet Week Four ~ Friday:

These are the things I love about myself:

_____

_____

These are the things I love about my partner:

_____

_____

These are the things I would still like to improve about myself:

_____

_____

These are the things I would like to improve in my relationship:

_____

_____

These are the things I will not change about myself for anyone:

_____

_____

_____

My greatest accomplishment today was:

_____

_____

The people I thought most about today were:

_____

_____

I could be a better lover if:

_____

_____

_____

When I think about my partner, the emotions I feel are:

_____

_____

_____

Use space below for additional notes:

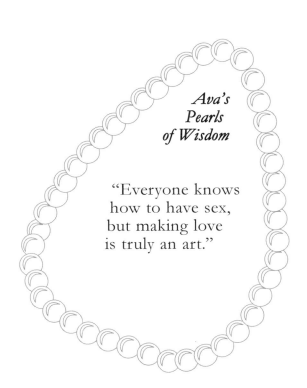

*Ava's
Pearls
of Wisdom*

"Everyone knows
how to have sex,
but making love
is truly an art."

Worksheet Week Four ~ Saturday:

Today my greatest strength was:

_____

_____

The most challenging part of the day was:

_____

_____

Here are 3 ways my relationship can improve and continue to grow:

_____

_____

_____

My most vulnerable moment was: Because:

_____

_____

What questions could I ask my partner to get to know her/him better?

_____

_____

_____

I know my life would be better if:

_____

_____

_____

_____

The one person I wish I could have spent more time with today was: Because:

_____

_____

_____

If I had more time today, I would have:

_____

_____

_____

What did I contribute this week to others?

_____

_____

_____

If I had to describe my day in one word, it would be:

_____

Use space below for additional notes:

Ava's
Pearls
of Wisdom

"No one regrets
being too generous,
but many regret
not being generous
enough."

Worksheet Week Four ~ Sunday:

Now, when I look in the mirror, I see:

_____

_____

_____

If I were stuck on a desert island and could only take one person that I know with me, I would bring? Because:

_____

_____

_____

If today were the last day on this planet, I would:

_____

_____

_____

Today my self-confidence was at its peak when:

_____

_____

_____

If there were one thing that I could repeat to do better, it would be:

_____

_____

_____

These are some of the emotions I experienced today (Use the emotional barometer):

_____

_____

_____

Write down what I told my partner (or date) that I wanted today.

_____

_____

Write down what I wanted from my partner (or date) that I did not ask for.

_____

_____

_____

_____

What commitments are most important in my life? (e.g. love, career, family, etc.,)

_____

_____

_____

_____

Use space below for additional notes:

Ava's
Pearls
of Wisdom

"The first one
to say,
'I'm sorry,'
is the winner."

30-Day Review:

The 30th day of the *12 Steps to Everlasting Love* is set aside for review. Look back on the journey of the last 4 weeks. This is my relationship/personal statement:

_____

_____

_____

What kind of party can I give to celebrate the completion of my 30-Day Plan-Of-Action?

_____

_____

How many new people have I met through my efforts on the 12 Steps to Everlasting Love?

_____

_____

How has my life changed in the past 30 days? What is the most valuable lesson I have learned?

_____

_____

How do I feel about myself, about my self-image and my confidence compared to when I first started this program?

_____

_____

How do I seem closer to my goal of finding an everlasting love relationship?

_____

_____

How will (or do) I know that my partner is my everlasting love?

_____

_____

A Note of Encouragement:

Don't despair if you have come to the 30th day without having found your everlasting love. You now have the tools to succeed, and you've learned to use them. Continue undaunted. Follow the program of Dr. Ava's 30-Day Plan-of-Action and the principles of Dr. Ava's 12 Steps to Everlasting Love and you will be successful.

♥ How would you feel if you found your everlasting love? You can use your emotion barometer if necessary to describe as many emotions as you can. (e.g. happy, secure, confident, loved, accepted, worthy, etc.)

_____

_____

_____

♥ Imagine yourself feeling this way everyday. This will help you remember what it is you want and who you want to be.

♥ If something doesn't go your way, stop and ask yourself how you could best handle the situation if you felt all the positive emotions on your list. What would you do differently?

Once you become more content with yourself and possess the self-confidence to compete in the avenues of romance, your wants and needs will be better defined and more easily obtainable. The context of social interaction may now be understood in a new light, thanks to the foundation of 12 steps upon which you have built your new persona.

Reflect on the progress that you have made since beginning to take an active role in your personal happiness. Applaud your own fortitude in sticking to Dr. Ava's 30-Day Plan-of-Action, and your dedication to the principles behind Dr. Ava's 12 Steps to Everlasting Love. Continue your daily and weekly exercises. Expand upon them. Expand your horizons to new and different social opportunities, and introduce others to the 12 Steps to Everlasting Love. There are some extra exercise sheets in the back for you to use.

Always look forward to the future and the hopes and dreams that await you will soon become reality!

Conceive it, believe it, and you will achieve it!

Positive Mirror Work

Look in the mirror. Which parts of my body do I associate with sex? Which parts of my body do I associate with displeasure and why? What would I like my body image to express to others (e.g. healthy, sexy, athletic)?

Date	Sex	Displeasure	Expressing My Healthy Body Image

Daily Positive Affirmation List

Remember, you have to love yourself first, before others can love you.

Date	Daily Positive Affirmation to Myself in Mirror

Personal Improvements

It is never too late to make self-improvements. Set target dates for yourself to start and complete each goal.

Date	Improvement/Goal	Future Result

New Friends Network

New People. Set a goal regarding how many people you are going to meet by this time next month. Make a date!

Date	Name	Phone	Where did you meet?	What did you admire about them?

Support System List

List what kind of support system will ensure your success. (a) Buddy System (b) Groups Meeting (c) Other.

Date	Support Type	Contact	Contact Phone	Result

Attraction List

Who am I attracted to? What do they look like and what are their qualities? What are the benefits of this relationship?

Date	Name	Phone	Where We Met	What I was Attracted to/Attributes I Liked

Social Life List

Where are you going to meet new people? List all the places you're going to go. Get creative!

Date	Place	Result

Risks List

What risks are you willing to take? Write down ways you will approach who you are attracted to. Take a chance because you have nothing to lose!

Date	Place	Risk	Result

Attributes of Others

Observe others. List the attributes you admired and would want to incorporate in your own style.

Date	Sex (M of F)	Attributes I Admired	How I Can Use It

Compliments & Criticisms

Remember that compliments are the bedrock of romance and constructive criticism can be a gift.

Date	Who	List Compliments & Criticisms From Others

Compliments & Praise

Compliment others physically, emotionally, mentally, and appreciatively on a regular basis.

Date	Who	List all the ways you can compliment and praise others.

Opening Lines List

What are you going to say? Write down three opening lines to begin a conversation with someone. Take a chance because you have nothing to lose!

Date	Place	Opening Line	Result

Enjoy Dr. Ava's
Books, Videos and Audio Cassettes

Love Around the House Book   AC-7900 $12.95
How to stimulate your love life with helpful household hints you won't find in any Martha Stewart book.

Between the Sheets Two Audio Cassettes   AC-6901 $19.95
Secrets of a sexologist for couples who want extraordinary sex.

Power of Seduction Video Tape (VHS)   AC-6900 $19.95
A live seminar on how to attract and become the perfect lover.

Stock Market Orgasm Book   AC-7901 $14.95
Enjoy a "Healthy Sexual Economy" by becoming a long term investor in love and enjoy the dividends of multiple orgasms for men and women.

12 Steps to Everlasting Love Workbook   AC-7902 $17.95
Discover how to move out of the past and into the future with a 30-day action plan to breakdown emotional walls and attract potential soul mates that lead you to live "happily ever after".

Confessions to A Sexologist Book   AC-7903 $19.95
Peeking into the sexual secrets of America. Covering such diverse issues as inhibitions, sexual etiquette, orgasm barriers, unusual outlets, and performance anxiety. This book will give you strategies to solve all your sexual concerns.

Passion Power Six Audio Cassettes, Workbook plus Stock Market Orgasm   AC-7904 $95.00
A personal fulfillment, sensual enrichment program that will bring passion back into your love life. And, if you already have passion, it's going to make it even better! It will improve intimacy and communication while expanding your sexual horizon.

Dr. Ava's Order Form

Product No.	Name of Item	Quantity	Price Each	Total

METHOD OF PAYMENT

☐ **Visa**   ☐ **Mastercard**   ☐ **Amex**   ☐ **Payment Enclosed**

Make checks or money orders payable to Kudos, Inc.

Credit Card Number _____

Expiration Date _____

Name on Credit Card _____

Signature _____

SHIP TO

Name _____

Address _____

City/State/Zip _____

Phone _____

Email _____

Cost of Materials	
Shipping & Handling (U.S. 10% with $5 min. Canada 20% with $10 min. Other 25% with $25 min.)	
Subtotal	
Sales Tax on Subtotal (California Only)	
TOTAL DUE	

Credit Card Orders Call Toll Free
888-40-DR-AVA (USA only)
310-276-8623

Fax
310-273-4924

Online
www.avacadell.com
www.sexpert.com

Visit Dr. Ava's Websites

www.avacadell.com

www.sexpert.com

The Best of Dr. Ava
Seminars, lectures & workshops
customized for your organization or group

12 Steps to Everlasting Love - **For Men & Women**
Discover how to move out of the past and into the future, breaking down the walls that have kept you from finding everlasting love. Learn how to take control of your own needs by focusing on your inner power. You'll also get a 30-day action plan to attract potential soul mates in order to live "happily ever after".

The Secrets of Seduction - **For Singles & Couples**
I'll show you how to heighten your senses, increase your perceptions, and prepare for sensual pleasures far beyond what you ever thought possible. Expand your sexual horizon with fantasy and creative foreplay. Rekindle the flame of passion in your relationship and create lasting romantic memories.

The Art of Erotic Dialogue - **For Singles & Couples**
I invite you to explore the mysteries of the language of love and learn a system so powerful that it will allow you to communicate your most intimate feelings without embarrassment or fear of rejection. You can open up doors of communication that may have been closed for too long and discover that erotic dialogue equals power.

How to Turn Your Man Into Putty - **For Women Only**
This class is for women who love romance and women who want to know more about sex. You'll learn how to become the seductive, wildly desirable person you've always dreamed of being. Discover secret erogenous zones that'll drive your man wild and turn him into putty in your hands.

What Women Really Want In Bed - **For Men Only**
This class is for men who want to be the best lover they can be. In this no-holds-barred seminar you'll discover what women wish you knew about them but rarely tell you. Find out how to really satisfy your lover with hot, safe and sexy techniques designed to empower you and satisfy any woman.

Stock Market Orgasm - **For Singles & Couples**
You will enjoy a "healthy sexual economy" with the "ups" and "downs" of the Stock Market Orgasm. We begin our investment journey with a "buy-in" to the future using components of flirting and caresses, ultimately exercising "options" such as G-spot stimulation and multiple orgasms for men nd women. Let the "profit" taking begin!

Business Principles Applied to Romance - **For Men & Women**
True success in business requires a synergy of mind, body and spirit and so does a successful relationship. In this class you will learn to balance your work life with your love life. Find out how to take principles such as time management and negotiation from the boardroom into the bedroom. Discover the connection between success and sexcess.

Passion Power - **For Couples**
A personal fulfillment, sensual enrichment program that will bring passion back into your love life. And, if you already have passion, it's going to make it even better--make your love life sizzle with spice and various new and exciting sexual and sensual adventures. Learn how to improve your communication, enhance your intimacy, and expand your sexual horizon.

NOTES

NOTES

NOTES

NOTES

NOTES

NOTES

NOTES

NOTES

NOTES

NOTES

NOTES

NOTES

NOTES

NOTES

NOTES

For More Information

on Dr. Ava Cadell's books, videos, audios, seminars, catalog or private practice, call:
(888) 40-DR. AVA (from USA only)
or (310) 276-8623

♥

or write to her office at:
9000 Sunset Blvd., Suite 1115, Los Angeles, CA 90069

♥

or contact her via fax, e-mail, or on the web
Fax (310) 273-4924
E-Mail DrAva@avacadell.com
www.avacadell.com
www.sexpert.com